Preface

I wrote in the Preface to the previous edition of this work, published in the shadow of the Housing Act 1996, 'Security of tenure is all but dead'. Nothing that has happened in the last four and a half years to provide encouragement from the point of view of the tenant.

Indeed, from the point of view of the substantive law, the area has not been a particularly fruitful one. The vast majority of cases involving Housing Act tenancies that reach the courts now are 'straightforward' possession actions. With the landlord's automatic entitlement to possession after six months, even arguments as to whether suspension of an order in rent arrears cases is appropriate are rarely meaningful.

In fact, it is seemingly arcane area of registered rents under the Rent Act 1977 that has attracted the most high profile litigation. A large number of these tenancies do survive, providing reasonably to secure housing to - now - relatively old people, and several thousand applications for rent registration are still made each year. A number of judicial decisions have required rent officers and rent assessment committees to assess rents more in line with market rents. The government's attempts to protect a vulnerable section of the population from the harshness of market forces was represented by Regulations, which put a cap on increases. These were ruled *ultra vires* by the Court of Appeal but were finally upheld by the House of Lords in December 2000 in *R v Secretary of State for the Environment ex p Spath Holme Ltd* [2001] 1 All ER 195.

The changes covered by this book have though been predominantly procedural, particularly the introduction of the CPR. Writing nearly two years after its introduction, one is beginning to get a proper feel of how it works. There is though little consistency between the courts as to how it should be applied. The hotch potch of Rules, Practice Directions, Protocols and Schedules retaining old CCRs and RSCs mean, for all its aspirations to simplicity, that it has proved to be one of the most cumbersomely drafted provisions English law has ever seen. Nonetheless it has probably just about been a success and we are moving towards a cheaper and quicker system of justice – something which in practice shifts the balance between landlords and tenants yet further towards landlords. I have tried to reduce the relevant Rules, where they touch upon the landlord and tenant field, to a reasonably comprehensible form. In this work I have also given more emphasis to the Gas Safety and Furniture and Fitting Regulations than I have in the past. These topics are treated disdainfully, if at all, by the writers of most work on the subject. They may not be of a great deal of academic interest, but to those who actually rent properties they are of the utmost importance and should be so to their advisers. Someone letting residential property for the first time may well not be aware of this legislation. If he seeks the advice of a solicitor on letting the property, is not told of these Regulations and is subsequently prosecuted for not complying, it is hard to see what defence to a negligence action the solicitor would have.

Time has marched on since the repeal in 1989 of the Rent Act 1977 in respect of new tenancies. Registered rents aside, tenancies under the 1977 Act become less significant as a topic. I have therefore omitted shorthold tenancies under that Act, and virtually omitted restricted contracts, though I am aware that a least a few of the latter remain.

My colleague Mark Loveday has perused the draft of my text, and I am grateful for a number of helpful suggestions, especially in the field of rent registration, where he has unparalleled expertise. As well as the author's customary acceptance, after acknowledging another's help, that all errors are his own, I perhaps owe it to Mark to make clear that his professional input should not be equated with any expressions of approval of non-legal opinion that might be found in the work. I – and perhaps even more so my publishers – am also grateful to another colleague, Helen Jefferson, for the assistance she has given me in chronicling changes to the law between preparation of the text and production of proofs.

Finally my family. Sarah, who was a very new born when I wrote the last edition, has reached a stage where she can advance promisingly sophisticated arguments about why Daddy's computer should be used to view Thomas the Tank Engine CDs rather than 'boring writing'. With younger siblings, James and Melanie, acting as her juniors, they made a formidable team presenting this case, which had ultimately to be rejected on economic grounds, attractive though it was. Had it not been for my wife Emma's efforts as usher, and indeed sometimes security guard, on my study door, I doubt the book would ever have got written at all.

Richard Colbey
2001

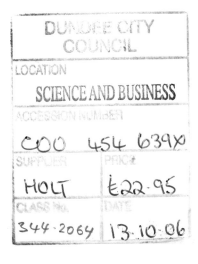

CAVENDISH PRACTICE NOTES

Residential Tenancies

FOURTH EDITION

RICHARD COLBEY
BARRISTER

SERIES EDITOR
CM BRAND, SOLICITOR

Cavendish
Publishing
Limited

London • Sydney

Fourth edition first published in Great Britain 2001 by Cavendish Publishing Limited, The Glass House, Wharton Street, London WC1X 9PX

Telephone: +44 (0)20 7278 8000   Facsimile: +44 (0)20 7278 8080
Email: info@cavendishpublishing.com
Website: www.cavendishpublishing.com

Colbey, Richard
Residential Tenancies – 4th edn – (Practice notes series)
1 Landlord and tenant – England   2 Landlord and tenant – Wales
I Title
346.4'2'0434

ISBN 1 85941 452 4

Printed and bound in Great Britain

Contents

1 Basic Information

1.1 Introduction

The book aims to be a concise guide to the law and practice of residential tenancies. The constraint of space has necessitated careful selection of the material so that discussion of some tenancies which could be regarded as falling within this field has been omitted. In particular, those seeking enlightenment on public sector tenancies, long leases and agricultural residential tenancies, to name the most significant omissions, will have to look elsewhere, although I hope this book will at least have been of assistance in telling them where to look. The statutory law which forms the backbone of the subject matter of this book was substantially overhauled by the Housing Act (HA) 1988, which applies to all private sector residential tenancies granted on or after 15 January 1989. This in turn was amended by the Housing Act 1996, which applies where the tenancy was granted on or after 28 February 1997. Neither of these Acts has retrospective effect. Therefore, the earlier legislation, largely contained in the Rent Act (RA) 1977, still remains important, as most tenancies granted before 1989 are still governed by it. I did hesitate to include the law relating to tenancies granted at least 12 years ago. However, I find in practice that I am still being instructed in a considerable number of problems arising out of pre-1989 tenancies. Indeed, because these tenancies are valuable assets to many tenants, in a way later tenancies are not, they do lead to more closely fought litigation, and while perhaps not numerically terribly significant, they provide a disproportionate amount of work for lawyers working in the field. In this book, I have dealt with each set of statutory codes, though with a greater emphasis on the later legislation. The book will, therefore, I hope, be useful for many years in dealing with problems arising out of both pre-HA 1988 and post-HA 1988 tenancies.

1.2   Sources

1.2.1   Statutes

Residential landlord and tenant law derives mainly from statute. The principal legislation is contained in the HA 1988. This Act had the effect of repealing the RA 1977 in respect of all but a tiny handful of new tenancies. It laid down a scheme of security of tenure and (very limited) rent control. It was a reflection of the Conservative Government's wish to eradicate legal control of the private sector housing market. A stated aim behind its introduction was to encourage more investment in the private sector, thus making more housing available. The aim has probably succeeded in as much as there is a greater degree of reasonable quality rented housing available for young working people, most of whom do not see themselves as having a long term future in the rented sector. The private sector, however, is increasingly becoming an irrelevance to those at the bottom end of the market. While the growth of housing association tenancies, which are generally covered by the same legislation as the true private sector, has gone some way to counter the eradication of local authority housing, most people on low incomes or benefits do not even think of properties owned by private landlords as an option any more.

The RA 1977, the last in a long series of Rent Acts, sets out the tenant's right to security of tenure and the fair rent provisions. That Act was significantly amended by the Housing Act 1980 and, to a lesser extent, by the Housing Act 1985. It still applies to all qualifying tenancies granted before 15 January 1989. The Protection from Eviction Act 1977, which, in many particulars, was strengthened by the HA 1988, gives both tenants and other residential occupiers protection from being evicted other than through the courts. In particular, the HA 1988 gave a statutory right to damages where a breach of the tenant's protection under the Protection from Eviction Act 1977 leads to him giving up his home.

The main effect of the HA 1996 was to make all new tenancies, by default, assured shorthold tenancies, which means that tenants have no statutory security of tenure after the initial six month period. As landlords could achieve the same result by specifically making earlier tenancies assured shortholds, and as, in respect of later ones, the parties are theoretically free to agree that the tenancy is not an assured shorthold, this was, in a sense, little more than a procedural change.

1.2.2 Secondary legislation

The relevant secondary legislation deals mainly with forms and procedure. There are a number of notices in connection with granting or terminating tenancies that have to be served in a prescribed form. Some of these are set out in Chapter 7 of this book. The statutory instruments are set out in full in all the main works on landlord and tenant law (see below, 11.1). Many of the instruments pertinent to residential tenancies are also contained in the Landlord and Tenant and Housing section of the Civil Court Practice (as the old County Court Practice 'Green Book' has become).

1.2.3 Case law

There are some areas which are not touched on by statute at all. Notable amongst these is the vexed question of whether a particular agreement is a tenancy or a licence. The most important cases are reported in the major law reports and in a number of other reports specialising in property matters (see below, 10.3).

1.3   Outline of the statutory provisions

1.3.1 Tenancies granted before 15 January 1989

The RA 1977 (to which most residential tenancies granted prior to 15 January 1989 are subject) provides an elaborate scheme for the assessment of fair rents and security of tenure for residential tenants. The legislation generally applies where the occupier is a tenant rather than a licensee. In *Street v Mountford* [1985] AC 809, the House of Lords reiterated that the principal test for determining the status of whether or not a residential occupier is a tenant is whether or not he has exclusive possession: if he does, he can qualify as a tenant. That test has, to some extent, been qualified by subsequent authority and, as explained in 2.1 below, exclusive possession will not suffice in every case. During a residential tenant's contractual term, he is known as a protected tenant. At the end of that contractual term, he will become a statutory tenant. Certain tenancies are excluded from being protected or statutory. These are listed in ss 4–16A of the RA 1977. Protected and statutory tenants have, except in prescribed circumstances, security of tenure, which overrides any contractual right to possession the landlord may have. These circumstances can relate to the tenant's own misconduct or, for example, the fact that the landlord requires the property for his own residence. If possession is sought on those grounds, the court has a discretion in deciding whether or not to order possession. Most of the provisions that give the court a discretion to order possession are contained in Pt I of Sched 15 to the RA 1977.

A landlord will have a right to possession where the premises have been used, or were intended, for one of a number of specified purposes before the tenancy commenced and the tenant was told of this in writing before the tenancy commenced and the property is now required for that purpose. The provisions that give the landlord this automatic right to possession are contained in Pt II of Sched 15 to the RA 1977. A landlord who wished to be sure of obtaining possession could grant a protected shorthold tenancy. This had to be for a term between one and five years, and the tenant had to be given a notice in the prescribed form before its commencement. Once the term expired, Case 19 of Sched 15 gave the landlord a right to recover possession so long as he followed the correct procedure. That right continued, even if the tenant were allowed to remain in occupation after the expiry of the agreed term.

Part IV of the 1977 Act provides for a system of registration of 'fair rents'. Either a residential tenant or landlord may apply to the rent officer to assess a figure for the maximum rent payable for the premises. This figure historically has tended to be well below the market rent. The right to make this application to the rent officer cannot be excluded by an agreement between the landlord and the tenant.

An important qualification of the scheme of security of tenure and rent control exists where there is a tenancy, but it is excluded from protection because the landlord is resident in the same building as the tenant, or board is provided for the tenant: then there will be a restricted contract rather than a tenancy. Some licences where the licensee has the right to occupy exclusively part of the premises will also be restricted contracts. There is a limited amount of security of tenure and rent control available to such licensees. However, the effluxion of time since the passing of the HA 1988 has rendered this all but obsolete.

1.3.2 Tenancies granted on or after 15 January 1989

The HA 1988 provided a rather more rudimentary scheme for giving tenants security of tenure and a limited right to have a rent determined independently of the agreement between the landlord and the tenant. These parts of the Act apply only to tenancies rather than to licences. During a tenant's contractual term, he is an assured tenant. At the expiry of that term, he becomes a statutory periodic tenant. Certain tenancies are excluded from being assured or periodic statutory tenancies. These are, for the most part, similar to those which are excluded from being protected or statutory tenancies under the RA 1977 and are listed in Sched 1 to the HA 1988. Excluded entirely from security of tenure and rent assessment provisions of the HA 1988 are agreements that would have been regarded as restricted contracts under the RA 1977, because the landlord was living in the same building as the tenant. Assured or periodic statutory tenants can be evicted only on certain grounds (some discretionary and some mandatory), which are listed in Sched 2 to the HA 1988. There is some, but far from complete, overlap with the circumstances in which a protected or statutory tenant can be evicted. Some grounds relate to the tenant's misconduct, including mandatory grounds where the tenant has been particularly recalcitrant in paying rent. Some grounds are dependent on a notice having been served before the commencement of the tenancy.

Under the 1988 Act, a tenant is not entitled to have any independent assessment of the rent when the tenancy is granted. Once the landlord wishes to raise the rent, he must first serve the tenant with notice of his intention of doing so. The tenant has the right to refer the contract to a rent assessment committee, which will prevent the landlord raising the rent to, in effect, more than the ordinary market rent of that property.

1.3.3 Tenancies granted on or after 28 February 1997

The HA 1996 reduced still further the protection of tenants. Section 9 of that Act provides that, from 28 February 1997, all new tenancies will be assured shortholds unless the parties expressly agree otherwise. This, in contrast to the transitional provisions in the HA 1988, applies to renewals of old assured shorthold tenancies after that date. Tenancies subject to the RA 1977 still retain their protection even if renewed after February 1997.

1.4   Glossary

Assured shorthold tenancy	Either (a) a tenancy first granted between 15 January 1989 and 28 February 1997 inclusive that would otherwise have been an assured tenancy, in respect of which an appropriate notice was served, or (b) a tenancy first granted on or after 28 February 1997

unless the parties agree – usually accomplished by the landlord serving a notice on the tenant before the tenancy begins – that it was not to be an assured shorthold.

Assured tenancy

A residential tenancy granted on or after 15 January 1989, which is not excluded from being such a tenancy. The term was also used to describe a few pre-HA tenancies granted by specified landlords, of premises newly built or substantially reconstructed, in respect of which a notice saying it is an assured tenancy was served on the tenant before commencement of its term (s 56 of the HA 1980). These are now subject to the same regime as assured tenancies under the HA 1988.

Break clause

A provision in a tenancy that enables either the landlord or the tenant to terminate it before the term expires.

Company let

The letting of residential premises to a company is usually described this way. Sometimes, particularly with pre-HA tenancies, it was used by landlords as a device to avoid tenants' statutory protection.

Dwelling house

The unit of property that can become the subject of a protected tenancy, statutory tenancy, assured tenancy or periodic statutory tenancy. In effect, it means a home. It can certainly include units such as flats and 'bedsits' which are not normally regarded as houses.

Excluded tenancy or licence

A tenancy or licence where the tenant or licensee has the use of any accommodation in common with the owner or a member of the owner's family, who occupied the premises as his only or principal home both at the beginning and end of the tenancy or licence (s 3A of the Protection from Eviction Act 1977). Such tenancies and licences are excluded from a number of the provisions preventing possession being recovered without due process of law.

Fair rent	The rent assessed by the rent officer when an application is made to register a rent in respect of a regulated tenancy.
Forfeiture	A landlord's common law right to re-enter the property if the tenant is in breach of a covenant of a tenancy agreement. A right to forfeiture can arise only out of an express covenant allowing forfeiture contained in the tenancy agreement. There are substantial restraints put on a landlord's power to exercise his right to forfeiture.
Ground rent	A rent paid by a lessee to the freeholder under a long lease for which the tenant has paid a substantial initial premium; usually this rent is of a nominal annual amount.
Lease	An agreement under which someone agrees to let another have exclusive possession of a property. Colloquially, though not in strict legal theory, tends to be reserved as a description for longer agreements.
Licence	A personal permission to occupy land, whether in exchange for payment or not. This does not give the licensee the rights of a tenant.
Mesne profits	A sum payable by a trespasser in a property in lieu of a rent. Where a court has made an order evicting a tenant, but allows him to remain in occupation for a period, he will no longer be a tenant, but technically a trespasser, and hence liable to pay mesne profits rather than rent. Although, strictly speaking, commencing proceedings does not bring a statutory tenancy to an end, it is usual practice to refer to sums which will be payable by the tenant in respect of his occupation of the premises after termination as mesne profits.

Notice to quit	A notice given by a landlord or tenant purporting to terminate a tenancy. In the case of a periodic tenancy or licence of a dwelling house, the landlord must give the tenant at least 28 days' notice of termination notwithstanding anything in the tenancy agreement allowing shorter notice to be given (s 5 of the Protection from Eviction Act 1977). In respect of assured tenancies, this notice has been replaced by the notice provided for in s 8 of the HA 1988.
Periodic statutory tenancy	The tenancy that will arise after the expiry of the contractual term of an assured tenancy (s 5 of the HA 1988), sometimes merely called a 'statutory tenancy'.
Premium	A payment made by a tenant in consideration of the grant or assignment of a tenancy. For residential tenancies where a market rent is paid, these are normally not required. The substantial payment, in practice regarded as the purchase price, made when someone buys a long lease on a flat, is a premium.
Protected shorthold tenancy	A tenancy granted before 15 January 1989 that would otherwise have been a protected tenancy, but which is granted for a fixed term of between one and five years in respect of which a notice telling the tenant it is to be a shorthold tenancy has been served (s 52 of the HA 1980).
Protected tenancy	A tenancy of a dwelling house during its contractual term (s 1 of the RA 1977).
Reasonable rent	The rent assessed by the rent tribunal when an application is made to register a rent in respect of a restricted contract.
Registered rent	The fair rent assessed by the rent officer in respect of a protected tenancy or statutory tenancy or the reasonable rent assessed by the rent tribunal in respect of a restricted contract.

Regulated tenancy	The generic term for protected tenancies and statutory tenancies (s 18 of the RA 1977).
Rent Assessment Committee	The panel, usually consisting of three members, which hears appeals from assessments of fair rent by the rent officer (s 65 of the RA 1977) and applications for determination of a proposed rent increase in respect of assured tenancies under the HA 1988 and assessing rents under assured shorthold tenancies under the HA 1988.
Rent officer	The officer given statutory authority over various matters concerning rent: most importantly, the assessment of fair rents (Pt IV of the RA 1977).
Restricted contracts	An agreement entered into before the commencement date of the HA 1988 under which a person is allowed exclusively to occupy a dwelling house, but which is not a protected tenancy because the lessor is resident or because the lessee is provided with board (s 19 of the RA 1977).
Secure tenancy	A tenancy that would otherwise be a protected tenancy, but which is granted by a specified public or charitable body to one or more individuals whose main residence the demised premises will be. Most council houses are let on secure tenancies (s 79 of the HA 1985).
Shorthold tenancy	See Assured shorthold tenancy and Protected shorthold tenancy.
Statutory tenancy	The tenancy that will arise once the contractual protected tenancy has come to an end. Alternatively, if a protected tenant dies, certain of his relatives, if they were residing with him in the dwelling, may become statutory tenants (s 2 of the RA 1977). Can, though rarely is, also be used to describe the tenancy that arises when an assured tenancy finishes.

Waste

Acts or omissions by a tenant that cause damage to the demised premises. Waste is either voluntary if it is active, for example, pulling down a wall, or permissive if it is passive, for example, failing to carry out necessary repairs.

2 The Nature of the Agreement

Since the coming into force of the Housing Act (HA) 1988, there have been two different regimes for determining the nature of tenancies. Tenancies granted before then are still subject to the Rent Act (RA) 1977 and/or the HA 1980 and later ones are subject to the provisions of the HA 1988, as amended by the HA 1996. Many pre-HA 1988 tenancies remain in existence and, for the moment, it remains important for the practitioner to be able to ascertain whether or not a tenancy granted prior to the HA 1988 is protected by the RA 1977. Some issues, though, such as whether or not there is a tenancy or a licence, apply equally whichever legislation was in force when possession was granted to the occupier.

2.1 The lease/licence distinction

The question of whether or not any agreement for the occupation of land amounts to a lease or to a licence is one that is very important in determining the relationship between the parties to that agreement. The distinction is particularly important in the residential sphere, as it determines whether or not the Rent or Housing Acts apply. It is not a distinction touched on at all by statute. The issue is more likely to arise in litigation relating to Rent Act tenancies, as the relative ease with which landlords can recover possession under the HA 1988 reduces the incentive to attempt to avoid the creation of a tenancy. The leading authority is *Street v Mountford* [1985] AC 809, HL. Mr Street had granted Mrs Mountford the right to occupy a furnished room under a written agreement which purported to be a 'personal licence'. Mrs Mountford had exclusive possession of the room. She applied to have a fair rent assessed in respect of the room. The rent officer had jurisdiction only if she were a tenant. The House of Lords eventually came to decide the issue. They decided in favour of a tenancy. Probably the most important points that can be extracted from Lord Templeman's opinion, which was the only substantive one given, were that:

(a) where exclusive possession of premises is granted to a person in return for payment there will, unless there are special circumstances which suggest the contrary, be a tenancy;

(b) the wording of any agreement the parties made was not crucial in determining whether or not exclusive possession had in fact been granted; and

(c) the courts should disregard the existence of the Rent Acts in deciding whether or not exclusive possession had been granted.

This decision makes it clear that property owners will not be able to avoid creating a tenancy by giving occupiers an agreement which purports to be a licence, but which is, in reality, a tenancy because exclusive possession has been granted. If the occupier is excluded from the premises for part of the day, he is unlikely to be a tenant (*Aslan v Murphy* [1989] 39 EG 109, CA). A mere gesture by the landlord towards retaining a right of occupation for himself, such as keeping a key, will not be sufficient to prevent there being exclusive possession (*Family Housing Association v Jones* [1990] 1 WLR 779, CA). In *Street v Mountford* Lord Templeman contrasted the tenant with a lodger, who does not have exclusive possession of any part of the premises, although he may exclusively occupy, for instance, one room. A lodger is someone, according to his Lordship (*Street v Mountford*, p 818A), for whom:

> ... the landlord [*sic*] provides attendance or services which require the landlord or his servants to exercise unrestrained access to and use of the premises. The whole of the agreement should be construed to decide whether or not the occupier was merely a lodger. Once it was established that he was not a lodger, if he were paying a regular sum in respect of his occupancy, whether or not described as 'rent', he would normally be a tenant. The position would be different only if there were special circumstances indicating that it had not been intended by the parties that he would occupy as a tenant.

Lord Templeman gave examples of these as occupancy under a contract to sell land or pursuant to an employment contract or where the parties had no intention to create legal relations at all. The Court of Appeal found that there were such exceptional circumstances in *Sharp v MacArthur* [1987] 19 HLR 364. There, the defendant had been let into possession of a house which was vacant and available for sale, having told the plaintiff that he was in dire need of accommodation. Although he paid a rent and was given a rent book, this was held not to amount to a tenancy. This decision may be of some comfort to property owners considering granting short-term 'licences' from altruistic motives. Nonetheless, it does not set such a clear precedent that one can safely advise that there will be no tenancy in the circumstances.

Authoritative though *Street v Mountford* is on the lease/licence distinction, it does not assist where there is an argument about whether or not exclusive possession has actually been granted. The Court of Appeal has held that it is wrong for a judge simply to ask himself whether a residential occupier is a tenant or a lodger without first considering the question of exclusive possession (*Brooker Settled Estates v Ayres* [1987] 1 EGLR 500). This leaves open the possibility that property owners may be able to avoid (now) the HA 1988 by using agreements entered into independently with more than one occupier, allowing each occupier to live in the property in common with the other occupiers, but having exclusive possession of no part of it. Such an agreement had been held to amount to only a licence in *Somma v Hazelhurst* [1978] 1 WLR 1014, CA, a case which was expressly overruled in *Street v Mountford*. However, the overruling of *Somma v Hazelhurst* may be explained on the basis that the agreement there was clearly a sham. The occupiers there had been a cohabiting couple who, in reality, would not have been asked to share their room with anyone else even if one of them had left.

'Sharing agreements' were considered by the House of Lords in *AG Securities v Vaughan; Antoniades v Villiers* [1990] AC 417. The House overturned the decisions of the Court of Appeal in both of these cases. In *Antoniades v Villiers*, the agreement was considered to be a sham, as the occupiers were living together as husband and wife and it was inconceivable that the landlord would have required them to share with anyone else. However, in *AG Securities v Vaughan*, each of the four occupants entered into their respective agreements on different dates, for different periods and were paying different 'rents'. This agreement was genuine and the House held there could not be a joint tenancy granted to the four occupiers. These cases suggest that it will be much harder to impose a sharing agreement on a group of occupiers who approach the landlord together. Making the occupiers jointly and severally liable for each other's rent is likely to be fatal to any attempt to avoid a tenancy (cf *Mikeover Ltd v Brady* [1989] 3 All ER 618). In practice, it will often be difficult to draw up an agreement which avoids the grant of a tenancy. Certainly, the courts will not attach a great ᵈ of weight to clever drafting which attempts to hide the realiᵗ agreement. If a property owner does request his legal adviᶜ this, there can be no objection to trying to draft, for instance, a 'sharing agreement'. The owner, however, must be informed that there is no guarantee that such drafting will succeed. Even if it does, the owner may well face costly proceedings to establish that there is no tenancy. For an example of an agreement that has been held to create a licence, see *Stribling v Wickham* [1989] 27 EG 81.

2.2 The requirement of residence

2.2.1 Under the RA 1977

There can be a statutory tenancy of a dwelling house under the RA 1977 only so long as the tenant occupies it as his residence (s 2(1)). The Act does not, however, effectively define 'residence' (cf s 3(2) of the RA 1968, Rent (Restrictions) Act 1920). The residence must be by the tenant personally: the fact that a member of his family lives there will not suffice (cf *Richards v Green* [1983] 268 EG 443, where the tenant always intended to return, and *Brickfield Properties v Hughes* [1988] 20 HLR 108, CA, where the intention to return was merely contingent). Residence is a question of fact and degree. It is possible for a person to have more than one 'residence' (*Brickfield Properties*). Merely sleeping at a property for several nights a week will not necessarily make it one's residence (*Hampstead Way Investments v Lewis-Weare* [1985] 1 WLR 164, HL). The courts should have regard to whether the tenant carries on the majority of life's activities, such as eating, cooking, bathing, and socialising as well as sleeping at the property (*Kavanagh v Lyrondias* [1985] 1 All ER 560, CA). A temporary absence, even an extended one, will not result in a cessation of residence (*Tickner v Hearn* [1960] 1 WLR 1406; *Richards v Green*, above). However, where the tenant spends most of his life abroad he will not be able to claim to be resident in the premises (*DJ Crocker v Johal* [1989] 42 EG 103, CA). It should be noted that a protected tenancy subsists as such without the requirement of residence if the property involved is a 'dwelling house'. Only once the contractual term has expired and the tenancy is potentially statutory does the question of residence need to be considered.

2.2.2 Under the HA 1988

Under the HA 1988, which applies if the tenancy was granted on or after 15 January 1989, for a tenancy to be an assured one the tenant, or at least one of the joint tenants, must occupy the property as his 'only or principal home' (s 1(1)(b) of the HA 1988). This requirement applies to its becoming an assured tenancy in the first place, as well as when it subsequently may become a statutory periodic tenancy. It makes no difference in this context whether or not the tenancy is an assured shorthold. The requirement is similar to that imposed on public sector tenancies by s 81 of the HA 1985. Physical presence is not necessary so long as the tenant evinces some intention to return to the property by, for instance, leaving his furniture there (*Crawley BC v Sawyer* [1987] 20 HLR 98, CA). Cases decided under the Leasehold Reform Act 1967 where the words 'only or main residence' are used may also be of assistance.

2.3   Tenancies which were not fully protected under the RA 1977

A tenancy under which a dwelling house or a part of one was let prior to the commencement of the HA 1988 on 15 January 1989 as a separate dwelling is a protected tenancy (s 1 of the RA 1977), and remains so even if subsequently renewed after that date. This is subject to a number of exceptions, which are discussed below.

After the contractual term of a protected tenancy has expired, it will become a statutory tenancy (s 2(1)(a) of the RA 1977). A statutory tenancy can also arise on the death of the protected tenant (s 2(1)(b) of the RA 1977). Certain types of residential tenancies are, however, specifically excluded from being protected or statutory tenancies under the RA 1977.

2.3.1 Dwelling houses above certain rateable values

Generally, properties with rateable values on 1 April 1973 (or when it was first valued, if later) in excess of £750 (£1,500 in Greater London) cannot be subject to protected tenancies. Rates were not abolished until after the RA 1977 was repealed (at least in respect of new tenancies), so old rateable values are still relevant. The only exception is where the value did not exceed specified amounts when the property was first valued or other amounts during the revaluation in the spring of 1973 (s 4 of the RA 1977). In practice, very few rented properties exceed these values.

2.3.2 Tenancies at low rents

A tenancy is not a protected tenancy if the rent payable is less than two-thirds of the rateable value of the property on the 'appropriate day' (s 5(1) of the RA 1977). The appropriate day will be 23 March 1963 unless the property was first valued on a later day, in which case it will generally be the day it was first valued (s 25 of the RA 1977). Slightly different rules apply if, on the 'appropriate day', the value exceeded £200 (£400 in Greater London) (s 5(2) of the RA 1977). If a sum is payable by the tenant in respect of, for instance, rates, services or repairs it will not count as rent for these purposes (s 5(4) of the RA 1977). If no rent is paid, there will not be a protected tenancy (s 5(1) of the RA 1977).

The extent to which a landlord could avoid giving security of tenure by including in the tenancy agreement provisions to change the rent so as to deprive the tenant of protection has been the subject of academic speculation but little judicial authority until very recently, in *Bankway Properties v Penfold-Dunsford* (2001) *The Times,* 24 April. The Court of Appeal decided that a term in an assured tenancy agreement increasing the annual rent to £25,000 two years after the tenancy commenced. It had been found as a fact that that provision had only been included to enable the landlord to determine the tenancy when the tenant did not pay. The tenant was on housing benefit and it was known that he would not have the means to pay that figure, which bore no resemblance to what the property was worth in any case.

It would seem to follow from this that provisions which enable the landlord to reduce the rent to below the minimum required to make a tenancy a protected or assured tenancy will be similarly void, if the court is satisfied that it is a sham. Identical principles will apply regardless of whether the 1977 or the 1988 Act applies.

2.3.3 Dwelling houses let with other land

If a dwelling house is let with other land to which it is merely an adjunct, there will not be a protected tenancy (s 6 of the RA 1977). However, unless the other land consists of more than two acres of agricultural land, it will be taken as part of the dwelling house and will not prevent there being a protected tenancy (s 26 of the RA 1977).

2.3.4 Payments for board and attendance

Where a part of the rent for which a dwelling house is let is bona fide payable in respect of board or attendance, there will not be a protected tenancy (s 7(1) of the RA 1977). Board, which is the provision of meals, must be more than minimal if the tenancy is not to be protected. Provision of continental breakfast will suffice (*Otter v Norman* [1988] 2 All ER 897, HL), whilst merely providing hot drinks would probably not. Attendance includes personal services, such as cleaning and making beds. For the tenancy not to be protected, the sum fairly attributable to the attendance, having regard to the value of the attendance to the tenant, must form a substantial part of the whole rent (s 7(2) of the RA 1977). This provision is one that was sometimes used by landlords wishing to avoid the Rent Acts.

2.3.5 Lettings to students

A tenancy granted by a specified educational institution to students while they study will not be a protected tenancy (s 8 of the RA 1977).

2.3.6 Holiday lettings

A tenancy is not a protected tenancy if its purpose is to confer on the tenant the right to occupy the dwelling house for a holiday (s 9 of the RA 1977).

2.3.7 Agricultural holdings

A tenancy is not a protected tenancy if the dwelling house is comprised in an agricultural holding and is occupied by the person responsible for the control of the farming of the holding (s 10 of the RA 1977). These tenancies are subject to the control of the Agricultural Holdings Act 1986 and associated legislation.

2.3.8 Licensed premises

Where a tenancy of a dwelling house consists of or comprises premises licensed for on-sales of alcohol, there will not be a protected tenancy (s 11 of the RA 1977).

2.3.9 Resident landlords

Where the landlord was resident in the same premises as the tenant, there would usually be a restricted contract under the RA 1977. However, a restricted contract ceases to be such at all, and hence loses all statutory protection, on the first date there is a change in the rent on or after 15 January 1989. The law relating to restricted contracts is now for practical purposes obsolete (see 2.10).

2.3.10 Landlord's interest belonging to Crown, local authority, housing association or co-operative

There will not be a protected tenancy where the landlord's interest is held by the Crown (s 13 of the RA 1977), local authority (s 14 of the RA 1977), housing association (s 15 of the RA 1977) or housing co-operative (s 16 of the RA 1977). Each of these is defined in the appropriate section. Pre-1988 tenants of the latter three bodies have a different form of statutory protection (ss 79–117 of the HA 1985), which is outside the scope of this book.

2.4   Company lets

Only an individual is capable of 'residing' in a dwelling house (see 2.2.1 and 2.2.2). Therefore, if a property were let to a company, there would be no statutory tenancy (*Hiller v United Dairies (London) Ltd* [1934] 1 KB 57). A 'company let' could though be a protected tenancy during the contractual term and the fair rent provisions would then apply (*Carter v SU Carburettor Co* [1942] 2 KB 288). Sometimes, landlords have insisted on prospective tenants forming a company so that premises can be let to them without there being the possibility of a statutory tenancy. Although this device sometimes succeeds (see, for example, *Firstcross Ltd v East West (Import/Export) Ltd* [1980] 255 EG 355, CA), there is a danger that the tenant company will be deemed to have sub-let to the actual occupier, notwithstanding any prohibition against that which may appear in the tenancy agreement. The courts will not allow the device of a 'company let' to succeed if doing so would be giving effect to a pure sham. On the other hand, the mere fact that there has been an attempt to avoid the Rent Acts will not automatically lead the courts to treat an agreement as a sham (*Hilton v Plastile Ltd* [1989] 05 EG 94, CA).

The grant of an assured tenancy under the HA 1988 is conditional upon the tenant being an individual (s 1(1)(a)). The issues when a 'company let' is granted and the tenancy would otherwise fail under this Act are similar to those where the RA 1977 applies to the tenancy. However, landlords are far less likely to resort to this device, as there are more straightforward ways of preventing Housing Act tenants from having long term security of tenure.

2.5   Protected shorthold tenancies under the RA 1977

This type of tenancy, introduced by the HA 1980, enabled a landlord letting property under a tenancy that was otherwise protected to be sure of being able to reclaim possession when the contractual term came to an end. Case 19 of the RA 1977 effectively deprived the shorthold tenant of all non-contractual security of tenure. Such a tenancy had to be for a fixed term between one and five years and not to contain a clause entitling the landlord to re-enter prior to its termination except if the tenant is in breach of an obligation of the tenancy (s 52(1)(a) of the HA 1980). The landlord must have given the tenant notice that the tenancy is to be a protected shorthold tenancy before it was granted (s 52(1)(a) and (3) of the HA 1980). If the tenancy would be a shorthold one but for the landlord's failure to serve the proper notice, the court has a discretion to treat it as a shorthold tenancy in a possession action if it is just and equitable in all the circumstances to do so (s 5(2) of the HA 1980).

2.6   Assured shorthold tenancies under the HA 1988

As with the protected shorthold tenancy under the RA 1977, the landlord has an automatic right to possession at the end of the contractual term of an assured shorthold tenancy. To qualify, a tenancy granted before the commencement of the HA 1996 on 28 February 1997 had to be granted for a term certain of not less than six months (s 18(1)(a) of the HA 1988). Subsequent to the Act, all residential tenancies are assured shorthold tenancies unless they are excluded by the new Sched 7 to the 1996 Act (s 19A and Sched 2A to the HA 1988). The landlord can prevent the tenancy being an assured shorthold tenancy by the service of a notice to that effect, or the tenancy agreement can contain provision to that effect. However, a tenancy which replaces an existing assured tenancy will not be an assured shorthold unless the tenant serves a notice on the landlord saying it is to be an assured shorthold (para 7 of Sched 2A). The HA 1996 removed the requirement that an assured shorthold tenancy be for a minimum of six months. However, the landlord will not be able to claim possession unless there is another statutory ground for possession until at least six months of the tenancy have elapsed (s 21(5) of the HA 1988). A landlord who wants to be able to obtain possession in less than six months, perhaps because he is going abroad for a shorter period, and then wants to live in the property, should serve notice specifying that the tenancy is not to be an assured shorthold. All subsequent tenancies of the same or substantially the same premises will be deemed to be assured shorthold tenancies, unless the landlord serves a notice on the tenant telling him that is not the case (s 18(3) and (4)). There is a slightly more effective form of rent control available to tenants under assured shorthold tenancies than where the tenancy is the basic assured tenancy under the HA 1988 (see 4.4). However, the tenant does not have the security from being evicted that an assured tenant does.

2.7   Tenancies under the RA 1977 which are subject to the Part II Cases

Part II of Sched 15 to the RA 1977 lists a number of situations, referred to as 'Cases', where a landlord will have an unfettered right to recover possession from a protected or statutory tenant. The Cases in Pt II are dependent on the satisfaction of specified conditions before the grant of the tenancy. Most of these Cases are discussed below. Each of them depends upon a notice having been served before the relevant date. This is defined in Pt III, para 2 of Sched 15. For most tenancies, it will simply be the date of the tenancy's commencement.

2.7.1 Case 11: owner-occupiers

For this Case to apply, the landlord must have previously resided in the dwelling house. Before the relevant date (see 2.7), the landlord must give written notice to the tenant that possession might be recovered under this Case. A further condition is that the property must not have been let on a protected tenancy in respect of which a Case 11 notice was not served by that landlord since a specified date, which will usually be 8 December 1965. Failure to serve the notice in respect of either the current or a previous tenancy will not necessarily prove fatal to a landlord's possession claim. The court has a discretion to make such an order notwithstanding non-compliance with the notice provision if the judge considers it just and equitable in all the circumstances to do so. To obtain possession pursuant to Case 11, the landlord must satisfy further conditions at the time of seeking possession.

2.7.2 Case 12: retirement homes

The primary requirement of this Case is that the landlord intends to occupy the dwelling house as his residence at such time as he might retire from regular employment and has let the property before retiring. The requirements as to notice in respect of this and any previous tenancies of the property the landlord may have granted are the same as for Case 11 tenancies, and the court has a similar discretion to override these requirements. Also, the landlord must fulfil further conditions before being able to obtain possession.

2.7.3 Case 13: holiday accommodation

This Case applies where, within the 12 months before the commencement of the tenancy, the dwelling house had been occupied under a right to occupy it for a holiday. The tenancy which is subject to Case 13 must be for a term certain not exceeding eight months. Before a tenancy subject to this Case commences, the tenant must be served with written notice telling him that the Case applies and the court does not have a discretion to waive service of that notice.

2.7.4 Case 14: student accommodation

This Case applies where, within the 12 months before the commencement of the tenancy, the dwelling house had been subject to a tenancy which was prevented from being protected by s 8(1) of the RA 1977 because it was granted by a recognised educational institution to a student (see 2.3.5). The tenancy subject to this Case must be for a term certain not exceeding 12 months. Before a tenancy subject to this Case commences, the tenant must be served with written notice telling him that the Case applies. The court does not have a discretion to waive service of that notice. It is unlikely that there are any of the inherently relatively transient tenancies covered by this provision still in existence.

2.7.5 Case 15: accommodation for ministers of religion

This Case applies where a dwelling house is held for the purpose of being available for a minister of religion as a residence from which to perform his duties. The court will grant possession if satisfied that the property is required for that purpose. It is immaterial how long the tenancy subject to this Case was granted for. Before the relevant date (see 2.7), the tenant under this Case had to be served with written notice telling him that the Case applied. The court does not have a discretion to waive service of that notice.

2.7.6 Cases 16, 17 and 18: agricultural accommodation

Case 16 applies where the dwelling house has, at some time, been occupied by an agricultural employee under the terms of his employment and the current tenant has never been employed by the landlord and is not the widow of a person who was so employed. The court will grant possession if satisfied that the dwelling house is required for occupation by an agricultural employee of the landlord. Before the relevant date (see 2.7), the tenant under this Case has to have been served with written notice telling him that the Case applies. The court does not have a discretion to waive service of that notice.

2.7.7 Case 19: protected shorthold tenancies

This Case applies where the tenancy granted was a protected shorthold tenancy (see 2.5). To obtain possession, the landlord must follow the procedure which is prescribed within the Case.

2.7.8 Case 20: accommodation owned by members of the armed forces

For this Case to apply, the landlord must have been a member of the regular armed services both at the date when he acquired the property and also when the tenancy was granted. Further conditions must be satisfied at the time possession is sought. He must have served the appropriate notice on the tenant before the commencement of the tenancy and must not have granted any tenancies in respect of which such a notice was not served since acquiring the property. The court, however, has a similar discretion to waive the service of this notice as it does for Cases 11 and 12 (see above, 2.7.1 and 2.7.2).

2.8   Tenancies under the HA 1988 which are subject to the Part I Grounds as a consequence of notice given on their granting

Part I of Sched 2 to the HA 1988 lists a number of situations, referred to as 'Grounds', where a landlord will have an unfettered right to recover possession from a protected tenant. Some of these Grounds are dependent on the satisfaction of specified conditions before the grant of the tenancy. These Grounds correspond to some extent in form and substance to the Cases listed in Pt II of Sched 15 to the RA 1977 (see 2.7). It should be noted that there are a number of other grounds where the court must order possession, which are not related to the service of notice before the grant of the tenancy. Obtaining possession pursuant to all these Grounds is discussed below.

2.8.1   Ground 1: landlord's own occupation of the premises

Ground 1 applies either where the landlord (or at least one joint landlord) has occupied the premises as his principal home before the beginning of the tenancy or, when possession is being sought, the landlord requires the premises as his or his spouse's principal home. Not later than the beginning of the tenancy, notice must be served on the tenant telling him that the landlord may recover possession pursuant to this ground. The court does, however, have a discretion to waive a failure to serve this notice if it considers it just and equitable to do so. (Sample notices are given below, 8.3 and 8.4.)

2.8.2   Ground 2: possession required by a mortgagee exercising a power of sale

Ground 2 applies where a mortgagee, such as a bank or building society, under a mortgage of the property, which was granted before the tenancy, wishes to claim possession to enable him to exercise a power of sale. The Ground is available only where notice was served before the grant of the tenancy. The Act refers to such 'notice ... as mentioned in Ground 1'. It is not clear whether this refers to notice that possession may be recovered pursuant to Ground 1 or to Ground 2. (For sample notices see 8.3 and 8.4.) Commercial mortgagees would be well advised to, but surprisingly often do not, make the service of such a notice a condition for their giving permission to mortgagor borrowers to grant tenancies.

2.8.3   Grounds 3, 4 and 5: holiday accommodation, student accommodation and accommodation for ministers of religion

Grounds 3, 4 and 5 respectively are identical to Cases 13, 14 and 15 contained in the Rent Act 1977, which are discussed at 2.7.3, 2.7.4 and 2.7.5 respectively.

2.9   Tenancies granted on or after 15 January 1989 which are not assured tenancies

Residential tenancies granted on or after 15 January 1989 will generally be assured, or now more frequently assured shorthold, tenancies during their contractual term. At the expiry of that term they will become periodic statutory tenancies. These concepts are analogous in their form, if not their effect, to respectively protected tenancies and statutory tenancies (see 2.3). The tenancies which are excluded from being assured tenancies are listed in Sched 1 to the 1988 Act. These for the most part correspond to the tenancies which were excluded from being protected tenancies under the Rent Act 1977. Tenancies granted before the 1988 Act came into force are not assured tenancies (Sched 1, para 1); nor are tenancies granted to protected tenants of substantially the same premises as they occupied prior to the commencement date of the Housing Act 1988 (s 34 of the HA 1988):

* Tenancies of properties with high rateable values granted before 1 April 1990 are excluded on terms similar to those of s 4 of the RA 1977 (see 2.3.1) (Sched 1, para 2). Tenancies granted on or after 1 April 1990 are excluded where the rent exceeds £25,000 per annum. This change is a consequence of the abolition of domestic rates after that date (Reference to Rating (Housing) Regulations 1990 (SI 1990/434)).

* Tenancies at a low rent are excluded on terms similar to those of s 5 RA 1977 (see 2.3.2) (Sched 1, para 3).

* Tenancies of business premises which are subject to the Landlord and Tenant Act 1954 are excluded (see 9.3) (Sched 1, para 4).

* Tenancies of licensed premises are excluded on terms similar to those of s 11 of the RA 1977 (see above, 2.3.8) (Sched 1, para 5).

* Tenancies under which agricultural land exceeding two acres is let together with the dwelling-house are excluded (Sched 1, para 6).

* Tenancies of agricultural holdings are excluded on terms similar to those of s 10 of the RA 1977 (see 2.3.7) (Sched 1, para 7).

- Lettings to students are excluded on terms similar to those of s 8 of the RA 1977 (see 2.3.5) (Sched 1, para 8).
- Holiday lettings are excluded on terms similar to those of s 9 of the RA 1977 (see 2.3.6) (Sched 1, para 9).
- Lettings by resident landlords are excluded on terms based on those of s 10 of the RA 1977 (see 2.3.9 and 2.10) (Sched 1, para 10). Where the tenancy is granted by joint landlords residence by any one of them will be sufficient to satisfy the requirements of this provision (Sched 1, para 10 (2)).
- Tenancies granted by the Crown are excluded on terms similar to those of s 13 of the RA 1977 (see 2.3.10) (Sched 1, para 11).
- Tenancies granted by local and certain other public authorities and fully mutual housing associations and housing action trusts are excluded (Sched 1, para 12).
- Tenancies which are the subject of various other legislation are excluded (Sched 1, para 13).

2.10 Resident landlords

Tenancies granted by resident landlords are generally excluded from full statutory protection, whether granted before or after the Housing Act 1988 came into force. Where the tenancy was granted on or after 15 January 1989, it will not be protected if, when the relationship of landlord and tenant first arose between the parties, the landlord's only or principal home was in the same building as the property let (Sched 1, para 2(b) of the HA 1988). Another flat in a purpose built block which is horizontally divided will not come within this provision, and there is then still potentially an assured tenancy (para 1(a)). The requirement of residence for a landlord in this context is the same as for a statutory assured tenant (see 2.2.2). The provisions which prevent there being a protected tenancy are dependent on the landlord's continued residence in the building. However, if a resident landlord assigns his interest to another person who then resides in the building, the tenancy will remain unprotected for 28 days (para 17(1)(a)). In that 28 day period, the assignee can either take up residence or serve written notice that he intends to do so within the next six months. As long as he takes up residence within six months, the notice will serve to prevent there being a protected tenancy. However, during any period when there is no landlord actually resident within the building, the courts can order possession only where grounds have arisen which would allow for the making of such an order against an assured or assured statutory tenant (para 21). There are further provisions which deal with the position where the resident landlord dies and/or his interest is vested in trustees (paras 18–20). Substantially similar provisions apply to tenancies subject to the RA 1977, though the requirement of residence is slightly different (see 2.2.1). These tenancies will be restricted contracts. Obtaining possession under a restricted contract is considered below, 6.10, but there are very few of these contracts left (see 2.3.9).

2.11 Tenancies not of land

It has recently been held that a permanently moored houseboat was not the subject of an assured tenancy (*Chelsea Yacht and Boat Co Ltd v Pope* [2000] 1 WLR 1941, CA). The Act only applies to lettings of land and, although the boat was classified as a dwelling, it was not annexed to the land to an extent that made it part of the land.

Similarly, lettings of mobile homes will not normally be subject to the Act, though a bungalow which could only be removed from land by being demolished will be, even in the absence of direct attachment between the land and the bungalow (*Elitestone v Morris* [1997] 1 WLR 687, HL).

The same principles would almost certainly apply had these cases fallen to be considered under the RA 1977.

3 Procedural Checklists

These checklists are provided to give practitioners an outline of what they need to do in frequently occurring situations. The lists should be read in conjunction with the relevant parts of this book and/or a more detailed work. Some obvious steps not specific to landlord and tenant matters, such as arranging funding with the client and/or applying for public funding aid and, where appropriate, instructing counsel, have been omitted from the individual lists.

3.1 Initial information to be ascertained on taking instructions from a landlord in connection with an existing residential tenancy

(1) A copy of the written agreement, if any, and any statutory notices that have been served.

(2) Name of the tenant and other occupiers (if any).

(3) Address and telephone number of premises.

(4) Name and address and telephone number of any solicitor acting for the tenants.

(5) Description of premises, for example, house, flat, bedsit.

(6) What services are provided?

(7) Is the landlord resident or absentee?

(8) Date tenancy was originally granted. (If it was before 15 January 1989, it will be subject to the provisions of the Rent Act 1977; if after that date it will be subject to the provisions of the Housing Act (HA) 1988. If on or after 28 February it will, unless notice to the contrary has been served, be an assured shorthold tenancy.)

(9) In the case of a tenancy first granted before 15 January 1989, is there a fair or reasonable rent already in existence for the property?

(10) What is the current rent?

(11) Does that rent include council tax, water rates, utility bills, services, anything else?

(12) When was the rent last altered?

(13) Is the letting furnished or unfurnished?

(14) Does the landlord own the freehold or is he a lessee himself?

(15) Is the landlord's interest subject to any mortgage?

3.2   Advising a landlord who wishes to grant a tenancy

(1)   Check information as in list 3.1 above.

(2)   If the landlord's interest is subject to a lease or a mortgage that restricts or prohibits sub-letting or letting, contact lessor or mortgagee to seek consent for the sub-letting or letting and, unless clearly instructed by the landlord that he wishes to proceed anyway, only proceed when and if this is obtained in writing.

(3)   Explain to prospective landlord the existence and effect of the HA 1988 security of tenure provisions and reference of rent provisions (see 4.4).

(4)   Ascertain whether any of the circumstances which enable a landlord to obtain possession as of right pursuant to Pt I of Sched 2 to the HA 1988 apply (see 2.8). In particular, if the landlord is an individual (rather than a company), ascertain whether he has ever lived in the premises or whether there is any possibility of him wishing to do so in the future. If that is the case, consider proceeding as in list 3.3, otherwise proceed to the step below.

(5)   Establish how long the landlord wishes the tenancy to last for. If it is less than six months, and one of the circumstances in (4) above applies, discuss the advantages and disadvantages of assured shorthold tenancies with the landlord (see 2.6). If the landlord wishes the tenancy to be an assured shorthold tenancy, continue as in list 3.4, otherwise proceed to the next step of this list and serve a notice saying that the tenancy is not to be an assured shorthold.

(6)   Discuss terms of tenancy with the landlord:

- Is it to be for a fixed period or renewable weekly, monthly, etc?
- What is the rent to be?
- Who is to pay council tax?
- Who is to pay water rates?
- What are the repairing responsibilities to be?

- Is the tenant to pay a deposit as security against damage to the premises and if so, who is to be entitled to the interest on that deposit?

- Is the landlord going to require the tenant to provide a guarantor for the rent?

- Are there any special terms?

- If there is a garden, is either the landlord or the tenant to be obliged to maintain it?

- Should there be a prohibition on large numbers of overnight guests and/or pets?

(7) Prepare tenancy agreement. An example of an agreement appears below, 8.1. Further terms can be added to that agreement.

(8) The landlord should be told to draw up an inventory of all fixtures, fittings, furniture and other items to be in the premises at the commencement of the tenancy.

(9) Ensure all tenants sign the agreement and inventory and pay any advance rent and deposit before the tenancy commences and that they are given keys to the premises.

(10) Ensure the landlord has obtained a gas safety certificate for the property (5.2), and that all the furniture complies with the Furniture and Fittings Regulations (5.3).

3.3   Granting a 'Ground 1' tenancy

This checklist can also be used where the tenancy granted is to be subject to one of the other Grounds requiring notice to be served before the commencement of the tenancy contained in Sched 2 to the HA 1988 (see 2.9). The endorsement on the tenancy notice in step (3) below must, of course, be adapted.

(1) Check initial information as in list 3.1.

(2) As in list 3.2, steps (2), (3), (6) and (10).

(3) Draft lease as in list 3.1 above. Endorse on lease notice that tenancy is to be subject to Ground 1 and, if the premises are subject to a mortgage, Ground 2 (see 8.3 and 8.4 for examples of such endorsements).

(4) The landlord should be told to draw up an inventory of all fixtures, fittings, furniture and other items to be in the premises at the commencement of the tenancy.

(5) Ensure all tenants sign agreement and inventory and pay any advance rent and deposit before the tenancy commences and that they are given keys to the premises. It is of particular importance to be in a position to prove that this notice was served on the tenants before commencement: the copy retained of the tenancy agreement should clearly indicate this.

3.4   Granting an assured shorthold tenancy

(1) Check initial information as in list 3.1.

(2) As in list 3.2, step (2).

(3) Explain to the prospective landlord the existence and effect of the HA 1988 provisions (see 4.4 for those specifically relevant to assured shorthold tenancies).

(4) Discuss terms of tenancy with landlord:

- What is the rent to be and when is it payable?
- Who is to pay water rates?
- What are the repairing responsibilities to be?
- Is the tenant to pay a deposit as security against damages to the premises and if so, who is to be entitled to interest on that deposit?
- Are there any special terms?
- If there is a garden, is either the landlord or the tenant to be obliged to maintain it?
- Should there be a prohibition on large numbers of overnight guests and/or pets?

(5) Prepare the tenancy agreement. This can take any form. The example given in 8.1 is suitable.

(6) The landlord should be told to draw up an inventory of all fixtures, fittings, furniture and other items to be in the premises at the commencement of the tenancy.

(7) The landlord should be told to draw up an inventory of all fixtures, fittings, furniture and other items to be in the premises at the commencement of the tenancy.

3.5   Advising a prospective tenant in connection with an assured tenancy

(1) Explain to the tenant about the rights and obligations of tenants under agreements of the type he is entering into are subject to, particularly the degree to which he will be entitled to security of tenure.

(2) Scrutinise the agreement proposed by the landlord to see if there are any particularly onerous terms. Is there a restriction on the number of people who may live at the premises? Is the tenant forbidden to keep pets?

(3) If the landlord is attempting to avoid the HA 1988 by the use of devices such as a 'licence' (see 2.1) or a company let (see 2.4), explain to the tenant about the likely effect of such devices.

(4) Advise the tenant about the existence of housing benefit (see 8.2).

(5) Advise the tenant to check carefully the contents of any inventory he is given before signing it.

3.6   Advising a client who wishes to apply for a fair rent

(1) Ascertain that the tenancy was granted before the commencement date of the HA 1988 and that, therefore, the client has the right to make the application.

(2) Explain to the client, whether landlord or tenant, about the advantages and disadvantages of a fair rent (see 4.2.1).

(3) Check that there is not already a fair rent in force for the property. Tenants are frequently ignorant of the existence of one. Landlords may also not know if they have recently acquired the property: it is not something that is checked by many conveyancers. If there is a rent registered more than three years ago, application can be made to change it (see 4.2.5).

(4) Obtain the prescribed application form from the local rent officer (they are generally listed in the telephone directory under 'Rent Officer') (RA 1977 (Forms etc) Regulations 1980 (SI 1980/1697), Sched 1, Form 5).

(5) Complete the form remembering that it is vital actually to specify the amount of rent the client is seeking to have registered. When taking the client's instructions on completing the form, it is advisable to take further details about the property, such as its size and general

condition, in case the rent officer makes further inquiries of the parties which have to be answered by you later.

(6)   Usually, there will be a hearing at which the parties will be able to discuss the amount of rent that should be registered. If attending that hearing, it is advisable to ascertain first the fair rents on a few apparently comparable properties: this can be done by checking the register the rent officer keeps. Also, prepare any arguments you may be able to muster as to why your property should have a higher or lower rent registered, such as its condition, size, situation and any special terms in the tenancy agreement.

(7)   On receipt of the rent officer's decision, notify the client, who then has 28 days to appeal to the rent assessment committee against the assessment if he is unhappy with it. An appeal can be commenced by notifying in writing the rent officer or rent assessment committee of an intention to object to the decision (see 4.2.4).

3.7   Acting for a landlord who wishes to terminate a pre-HA protected or statutory tenancy

(1)   Unless there is complete hostility between landlord and tenant, it is usually advisable to contact the tenant informally to see if he is willing to move, and to arrange a mutually convenient time for him to do so.

(2)   The appropriate notice should be served on the tenant. A notice to quit should be served on the tenant if he is still a protected tenant under the RA 1977. This must contain the prescribed information (for which, see 8.7). No notice to quit is necessary for a statutory tenant under the RA 1977. No proceedings for possession should be commenced until the notice expires. If a notice to quit needs to be served, premature commencement will be fatal to the landlord's case.

(3)   If a pre-HA tenancy, check whether the tenancy is subject to one of the Cases in Pt II of Sched 15 to the RA 1977 (see 2.8). If it is, and the appropriate notice was served before the commencement of the tenancy, the landlord will be able to use the procedures described in lists 3.9 and 3.10 below; otherwise proceed to step (4).

(4)   Issue proceedings for possession, in the county court. If the claim is based on arrears of rent, the correct form must be used (see 8.15). See below for advice on drafting the particulars of claim generally.

(5)   The landlord can be told that he will not prejudice his position by accepting rent from the tenant whilst awaiting trial.

(6)   If the defendant files a defence, consideration should be given to whether a reply is appropriate. If a counterclaim (referred to, post-CPR, as a 'Part 20' claim) is made, it is essential, unless it is admitted to serve a defence to a Part 20 claim.

(7)   Even if no defence is filed, the landlord should be able to call sufficient witnesses at the hearing to prove the case for possession (unless he was relying on the summary procedure in relation to a notice served before the tenancy commenced, in which case possession should be ordered automatically in the absence of a defence).

(8)   At the end of a successful hearing, an application for costs should be made, even if it is felt that it is unlikely that these will ever be recovered.

3.8   Acting for a landlord who wishes to terminate an assured tenancy

(1)   Unless there is complete hostility between landlord and tenant, it is usually advisable to contact the tenant informally to see if he is willing to move and to arrange a mutually convenient time for him to do so.

(2)   A notice must be served on the tenant informing him of the landlord's intention to take proceedings (see 8.13 for the prescribed form). Either two months' or two weeks' notice must be given, depending upon the Grounds for possession to be relied upon, unless the claim is based on Ground 14, nuisance or criminal activity.

(3)   Issue proceedings for possession, in the county court. If the claim is based on arrears of rent, the prescribed form must be used (see 8.15). If the claim is based on notice served before the tenancy commenced, then the abbreviated form of proceedings described at 5.8 can be used. The landlord will have to swear it, as it takes the form of an affidavit.

(4)   As in list 3.7, steps (4), (5), (6), (7) and (8).

3.9 Acting for a landlord who wishes to terminate a tenancy that is subject to a Case in Pt II of Sched 15 to the RA 1977

(1) As in list 3.8, steps (1) and (2).

(2) Ascertain whether circumstances that entitle the landlord to possession have arisen.

(3) If there is unlikely to be a dispute of fact, use the procedure prescribed in Pt 8 of the CPR 1998. Otherwise, use the procedure described in 3.7 above.

(4) If using the CPR Pt 8 procedure, complete and serve the claim form and supporting written evidence.

(5) The court will then direct a hearing or give such other directions as it considers appropriate in the light of whatever response the defendant has provided. There will usually have to be a hearing, even if the defendant does not respond to the application.

3.10 Terminating an assured shorthold tenancy

(1) Serve written notice on the tenant that the tenancy is being brought to an end. At least two months' notice must be given.

(2) Commence proceedings using the summary form of proceedings described in 6.8.

3.11 Evicting a residential occupier who is not a tenant

(1) Check that the occupier's contractual right to occupy the premises has expired or been forfeited pursuant to a term in the contract under which he occupies the premises.

(2) Ascertain whether the circumstances are such that the court is likely to refuse to award possession without a full trial (see 6.4), that is, against long standing occupants and where the occupier appears to have an arguable claim to be a tenant.

(3) Consider whether the case is one of urgency, for instance, the applicant is a displaced residential occupier (that is, someone who is unable to live in his home due to its unlawful occupation by another). If so, a return date less than the stipulated five days after service may be set.

(4) File the appropriate application (see 8.16 for the form) and an affidavit in support stating the applicant's interest in the land, the circumstances in which the licence is occupied without his licence or consent and that he does not know the name of any person occupying the land who is not named in the originating application (see 8.17 for an example).

(5) If all the defendants are known, seek leave to dispense with the measures indicated in step (7) below.

(6) Serve the application on all the known defendants.

(7) Affix a copy of each of the documents to the main door or other conspicuous part of the premises and, if practicable, insert through the letter box at the premises a copy of those documents in a sealed envelope addressed to 'The Occupiers'.

(8) If hearing date is less than five days after service, application for leave to abridge the period should be made at the hearing.

(9) As in list 3.7, step (8).

3.12 Acting for a tenant or licensee in a possession claim

(1) Ascertain from the tenant whether he particularly wishes to remain in the premises or would be prepared to leave on payment of a sum of money from the landlord.

(2) Contact the landlord or his representative to ascertain their position and conduct any appropriate negotiations.

(3) Advise the client on the merits of the landlord's case. If a device such as a 'licence' or 'company let' has been used, tell the client that he may still be a protected, assured or statutory tenant.

(4) If the landlord uses one of the summary procedures as in lists 3.9, 3.10 and 3.11, and there does seem to be an arguable defence to the claim, an affidavit in reply should be filed and served before the return date if possible; if there is insufficient time, the client should be prepared to give oral evidence at the hearing.

(5) If the county court fixed-date procedure is used by the landlord, then a defence and, if appropriate, a counterclaim should be filed. Particularly if the claim is on the grounds of non-payment of rent, the court should be asked to suspend any possession order that it may make.

4 Rent, Rent Control and Premiums, Terms of Tenancy and Statutory Rights of Succession to Tenancies

4.1 The obligation to pay rent

The amount of rent payable under any tenancy is primarily a matter for the parties to that agreement. Residential tenancies do not constitute an exception to that principle: landlord and tenant are free to agree any rent that they wish. However, where the Rent Act (RA) 1977 applies, either party has a right to ask an independent body to assess a fair rent (see 4.2 below) in the case of a protected or statutory tenancy, and a registered rent in the case of a restricted contract (although this last procedure is now virtually obsolete). Once such a rent has been assessed, the contract between landlord and tenant is overridden to the extent that that rent becomes the maximum payable. Where the Housing Act (HA) 1988 applies and there is an assured tenancy, there is no right to apply for a rent to be assessed on the initial granting of the tenancy, although there is such a right where there is an assured shorthold tenancy. The tenant may ask for the rent to be independently assessed on the renewal of the tenancy if the landlord wishes to increase it.

4.2 Applying for a fair rent in respect of a protected or statutory tenancy

The parties' right to apply to the rent officer to assess a binding 'fair rent' in respect of the demised property cannot be excluded by any prior agreement between the landlord and tenant (s 44 (2) of the RA 1977). The application can be made by either a protected or statutory tenant. Fair rents have historically been below market rents; sometimes, particularly in London, dramatically so. However, these reduced values were due to the fact that prior to the passing of the HA 1988 there was virtually no free market in residential rented property. Since that Act came into force, there has been a gradual increase in the rents assessed by rent officers, rent assessment committees and courts (see *Curtis v London Rent Assessment Committee* [1999] QB 92). The relevant legislation is contained in Pt IV, ss 62–75 of the RA 1977. The government attempted to introduce regulations that would mitigate the harshness of these increases for tenants by capping the increases (Rent Acts (Maximum Fair Rent) Order 1999 (SI 1999/6)). Despite a powerful argument, accepted in the Court of Appeal, that these Regulations were *ultra vires*, their validity was confirmed by the House of Lords in *R v Secretary of State for the Environment ex p Spath Holme Ltd* [2001] 1 All ER 195.

4.2.1 The advantages and disadvantages of a fair rent

Surprisingly few applications are made by tenants for fair rents to be assessed. This is probably a result of a combination of tenants' ignorance of the procedure, a desire not to upset their landlords and, perhaps in some cases, a feeling that having agreed to pay a certain amount it is wrong to attempt to pay less. Whilst these reasons may be entirely understandable, tenants should always bear in mind that a fair rent is likely to be less than the agreed contractual rent. Although there were sometimes advantages for a landlord who applied for a fair rent at the beginning of a tenancy (he would at least then know what the likely rent for the whole term would be), it would rarely be advisable for him to do so during the course of an established tenancy, where the rent had not already been registered. The only likely result would be a deduction in the amount of rent received.

4.2.2 The rent officer's jurisdiction

The rent officer only has jurisdiction to assess a rent if there is a tenancy and it is 'protected' within the meaning of s 1 of the RA 1977 (see 2.3). The fact that there is not a tenancy capable of becoming a 'statutory' tenancy because, for instance, the tenant is not resident (see 2.2.1) or is not an individual (see 2.4) will not affect the rent officer's jurisdiction. If the rent officer's jurisdiction is challenged by a party (most commonly this will be by the landlord claiming there is a licence rather than a tenancy), he may still determine a fair rent if he thinks it appropriate to do so (*R v Rent Officer for Camden ex p Ebiri* [1981] 1 All ER 950). If the rent officer is not willing to do so, the party making the application can apply by originating application to the county court for a determination of whether or not the tenancy is a regulated one (s 141 of the RA 1977, Rent (County Court Proceedings) Rules 1970 (SI 1970/1851), r 3(1)). Such an application should be made pursuant to Pt 8 of the CPR 1998.

4.2.3 Procedure for applying for the assessment of a fair rent

Section 67 of the RA 1977 provides that the application for the assessment of a fair rent can be made by the landlord, the tenant or both jointly. The application is made in the first instance to the rent officer. It must be on the prescribed form (s 67(2) of the RA 1977), which can be obtained from the rent officer (of whom there is one for each county council, London borough, metropolitan district or, in Wales, a county borough council). Completion of the form is very straightforward. It is essential that the question asking what amount of rent the applicant is seeking to register be answered. If this is not done, the application will be void (*Chapman v Earl* [1968] 2 All ER 1214). To avoid prejudicing their position, landlords are generally best advised to state what they believe to be the market rent (perhaps that presently being charged) and leave it to the rent officer to decide how much it has to be reduced. For similar reasons, tenants should state an unrealistically low amount, such as £5 per week.

After receiving the application, the rent officer can ask either party to provide further information. At the request of either party or at his own volition, the rent officer can hold a meeting for the parties, at which they can be represented by counsel, a solicitor or anybody else. The rent officer will listen to any arguments concerning the amount of rent that should be registered. Factors such as the size and condition of the premises can be referred to. Any particularly onerous or unusual terms in the tenancy agreement should be drawn to his attention. Normally the rent officer will inspect and measure up the premises. The amount of the fair rent that the rent officer has determined will then be notified to the parties.

4.2.4 Appeals against the rent officer's assessment

An appeal against the rent officer's decision is by way of a full rehearing of the application before a rent assessment committee. Such an appeal must be made within 28 days of the notification of the rent officer's decision to the parties. The appeal is made by writing to the rent officer giving notice of objection to his decision. A notice of appeal received after the 28 day period may still be entertained if either the rent officer or the committee exercise their discretion to do so (Sched 11, para 6(1) of the RA 1977). The committee has a power similar to that of the rent officer to request further information from either party (Sched 11, para 7(1) of the RA 1977). Non-compliance with a request of the committee without reasonable excuse is a criminal offence punishable by a fine (Sched 11, para 7(2) of the RA 1977). Usually, the committee will inspect the premises and hold an oral hearing. They must hold the hearing if either party requests it (Sched 11, para 8 of the RA 1977). The committee may either affirm the rent officer's decision or set a fair rent of their own (Sched 11, para 9(1) of the RA 1977). The committee could vary the rent upwards even if it were the tenant who appealed and downwards even if it were the landlord, a fact to which the attention of a party considering an appeal should always be drawn. There is a right of appeal to the High Court on a point of law against the committee's decision (s 11 of the Tribunal and Inquiries Act 1992). Rent assessment committees, like rent officers, are also subject to the supervision of the High Court by way of judicial review.

4.2.5 Effect of registering a fair rent

The consequence of the registration of a fair rent is that no greater amount of rent may be recovered by the landlord in respect of those premises (ss 44, 45 of the RA 1977). Where the fair rent is more than the contractual rent, the landlord may not increase the rent during the contractual term of the tenancy: paradoxically, an increase, though not a decrease, is regarded as a breach of the tenancy contract. Once the contractual term has expired, he may increase the rent up to the amount of the fair rent, but must serve a notice of increase (s 45(2)(b) of the RA 1977). This notice must be in the prescribed form (for which see the Rent Act 1977 (Forms etc) Regulations 1980 (SI 1980/1697)) (s 49(2) of the RA 1977). It must be served not later than 28 days after the increase is to take effect (s 49(3) of the RA 1977). A fair rent is effective only from the date on which it is first registered unless the rent is eventually determined by a rent assessment committee, when it is effective only from the date of their decision (s 72(1) of the RA 1977). It is therefore in the interests of the party hoping to benefit from the application to proceed as quickly as possible. If the application is the tenant's, it would not be exceptional for his rent to be halved. During the inevitable delay before the committee hears the appeal, he will have to continue paying the existing rent. This extra payment may cancel out any benefit he would gain from a reduction in the assessed rent, even if his appeal succeeds.

An application to vary the fair rent may be made at any time by either party on the basis that the circumstances appertaining to the property and/or the tenancy have changed so as to make the rent previously assessed no longer fair (s 57(3) of the RA 1977). Such an application should be made on the same form as is used for the primary application. Otherwise, the tenant may not apply for a new rent until two years have expired since the last registration. The landlord may apply after 21 months, although the new rent will not become effective until after the expiry of the two year period.

4.2.6 Factors taken into account in the determination of a fair rent

The legislation does not provide rent officers and rent assessment committees with any formulae to use in assessing the amount of fair rent to be registered. They are merely told to have regard to all the circumstances (other than personal circumstances) and, in particular, to the age, character, locality and state of repair of the dwelling house and, if any furniture is to be provided for use under the tenancy, the quantity, quality and condition of the furniture (s 70(2) of the RA 1977). Any scarcity of either would-be tenants or (far more significantly) property available for letting is to be disregarded (s 70(2)). Assured tenancy comparables may be taken into account, though the rent officer must not lose sight of the fact that security value will not have been disregarded in respect of them. It is not improper for a rent officer to disregard them altogether, though it will become increasingly impractical to do so (*Spath Holme Ltd v Greater Manchester and Lancashire Rent Assessment Committee* [1995] 49 EG 128, CA).

The best way to find out roughly how much a fair rent is likely to be in respect of any property is to consult the public register retained by the rent officer. The rents registered recently in respect of comparable dwellings will give a fair indication of the probable figure.

4.3 Rent control for assured tenancies under the HA 1988

4.3.1 The rent that can be charged initially on the granting of an assured tenancy

The Housing Act 1988 allows a landlord to charge whatever rent he is able to negotiate when a tenancy is first granted. This rent will remain payable so long as the initial contractual assured tenancy lasts. The 1988 Act is based on the free market principle of allowing the parties to strike their own bargain. Once the initial contractual term expires, the tenant may be entitled to remain as a periodic statutory tenant. The landlord is entitled to carry on receiving the same rent during that tenancy unless he wishes to increase the rent, in which case the protection described below is available to the tenant.

4.3.2 Action to be taken by a landlord wishing to increase the rent charged under an assured tenancy

The landlord may not increase the rent until the tenancy has lasted for at least 12 months, though he may serve notice of increase within that period (s 13(2) of the HA 1988). The notice of increase, in which the landlord 'proposes' a new rent, must be served on the tenant so as to expire after that 12 month date. In the case of a yearly tenancy, at least six months' notice must be given, otherwise a period of notice equal to the period of the tenancy must be given, subject to a minimum period of one month (s 13(3) of the HA 1988). The notice must be in the prescribed form (see 8.8). The rent increase proposed in the notice will then take effect automatically unless the tenant refers the matter to a rent assessment committee or persuades the landlord not to impose the increase (s 13(4) of the HA 1988). Many tenants do not appreciate the significance of the notice and will fail to take advantage of their right to refer it to the committee, thus allowing their rent to be increased by default.

4.3.3 Reference of a proposed rent increase to a rent assessment committee

The reference to the committee must take place before the notice of proposed increase has expired, otherwise the committee will have no power to consider it. (For information on the prescribed form of reference, see 8.9.) The committee determines the rent to be charged after the expiry of the notice of increase with reference to the rent they consider that the dwelling house concerned might reasonably be expected to be let in the open market by a willing landlord under an assured tenancy (s 14(1) of the HA 1988). The committee, in making that evaluation, is to assume that the hypothetical tenancy is for the same period and on the same terms (except for rent) as the tenancy they are actually considering. However, the committee is to disregard the effect on rent of the tenancy being granted to a sitting tenant, who might be prepared to pay 'over the odds' to preserve his home and also any extra-contractual improvements carried out by the tenant or deterioration caused by his failure to comply with the tenancy agreement (s 14(2) of the HA 1988). There is a significant contrast with the corresponding provisions under the RA 1977 in that the committee is not required to disregard any effect that scarcity of similar rented accommodation has on the amount of market rent. Normally, the rent decided upon by the committee will be backdated to the date of expiry of the notice (assuming they have been unable to assess it before that date). There is, however, a discretion where the tenant would otherwise be caused 'undue hardship' to postpone the coming into effect of the increase until any date up to that of the actual assessment.

4.4   Rent control for assured shorthold tenancies under the HA 1988

Where an assured shorthold tenancy is granted, the tenant has the right to make an application to the rent assessment committee to determine a rent. This may be done during the contractual term of the tenancy (s 22 of the HA 1988). The committee will be able to consider the application only if it considers there are a sufficient number of similar dwelling houses in the same locality (s 22(3)(a) of the HA 1988). The committee will consider whether the contractual rent is significantly higher than the rent which the landlord might reasonably be expected to obtain having regard to the level of rents paid under similar tenancies in the locality. The application has to be in the prescribed form (s 22(1) of the HA 1988). The rent assessed by the committee, if different from that charged by the landlord, shall be payable from such date as the committee may determine. It may not, however, be backdated to before the date of the application (s 22(4)(a) of the HA 1988). The statute does not seem to envisage the possibility of the committee determining a rent higher than the contractual rent. However, if such a rent were determined, there is nothing in the section that would enable a landlord to recover any amount over and above his contractual entitlement. An application may not be made for a determination of rent if the rent payable has already been determined by a rent assessment committee either in respect of an assured tenancy or an assured shorthold tenancy (s 22(2) of the HA 1988). If there is an assured shorthold tenancy granted after the commencement of the HA 1996, no application may be made after more than six months of that tenancy (s 22(2)(aa)). Once a rent has been determined under this provision, the landlord may not serve a notice of increase of rent until at least 12 months after the determination (s 22(4)(c) of the HA 1988).

4.5   Other statutory provisions relating to rent

4.5.1 Premiums and deposits

Although it was an offence under the RA 1977 to charge a premium for the granting of a protected tenancy, this does not apply to assured tenancies granted under the HA 1988. However, if such a premium is charged, the tenancy then becomes assignable, which is not otherwise the case (s 15 of the HA 1988).

4.5.2 Rent books

Where the rent is payable weekly by a residential occupier, except one for whom board is provided (see 2.3.4) it is a criminal offence for the landlord not to provide a rent book (ss 4, 7 of the Landlord and Tenant Act 1985). The book must contain prescribed information (s 5), which is specified in the Rent Books (Forms of Notice) Regulations 1982 (SI 1982/1474). Rent books in the correct form are obtainable from many general stationers.

4.5.3 Maximum charges for gas and electricity supplies

Maximum prices, which include a profit element, that the landlord may charge his tenant for gas and electricity are specified by the gas and electricity authorities by s 37 of the Gas Act 1986 and s 44 of the Electricity Act 1989. The authorities' respective councils will provide up to date figures.

4.6   Notification of the landlord's address and other information

Section 47 of the Landlord and Tenant Act 1987 requires landlords to state their name and address on any rent demand sent to tenants. If the landlord is not resident in England or Wales, the demand must also state an address at which notices, including notices in proceedings, can be served on the landlord. Section 48 of the 1987 Act further requires the landlord to provide the tenant with a notice giving an address in England or Wales at which notices can be served on him (see 8.6). If these provisions are not complied with, no rent or service charge is due from the tenant until the address is supplied (ss 47(2), 48(2)). An unqualified statement of the landlord's address in the tenancy agreement may suffice for the purposes of s 48 (*Rogan v Woodfield Building Services* [1994] EGCS 145, CA). Since the Housing Act 1996 came into force, the tenant can require the landlord to give him written notice of many terms of the tenancy not already reduced to writing (s 20A). This includes the amount of rent, the dates it is payable, provision for rent reviews, and length of the term if it is a fixed term tenancy (s 20A(2)). This provision seems to overlook the fact that a tenancy is supposed to be an agreement between two parties, with neither having more power to impose terms than the other. Although the section does say that the statement by the landlord will not be conclusive proof of the terms, it suggests that landlords should have greater power than basic contractual principles would suggest.

4.7   The effect on rent of the abolition of domestic rates

As from 1 April 1990, domestic rates were abolished in England and Wales by the Local Government Finance Act 1988, which introduced the ill-fated community charge. This was replaced in turn by the Local Government Finance Act 1992, which introduced council tax as from 1 April 1993. It is the tenant, rather than the landlord, who has the primary duty to pay council tax on a property (s 6(2) of the 1992 Act). Both Acts have been remarkably silent upon what the position is to be where the existence of rates had a bearing on the rent payable. It is arguable that a landlord who continued to collect the rates element after rates were abolished had increased the rent, which, where there is a tenancy subject to the HA 1988, he can do only if he follows specified procedures. Likewise, if the tenancy is subject to the RA 1977 and a fair rent has been assessed, the landlord cannot unilaterally increase it.

In those circumstances, the tenant would arguably be entitled to withhold the rates element.

Where the rateable value would have affected the status of a tenancy, this will now be determined by reference to the rent payable (see above, Chapter 2).

5 Obligations During the Currency of the Tenancy and Statutory Rights of Succession

5.1 Repairing obligations

The parties to a tenancy agreement are, to some extent, free to agree upon their respective repairing obligations. The extent of their respective obligations will be one of the circumstances taken into account by the rent officer in assessing a fair rent and, *mutatis mutandis*, by the rent assessment committee (see above, Chapter 4). However, statute implies a covenant that where there is a lease of a dwelling house for a period of less than seven years the landlord will:

(a) keep in repair the structure and exterior of the dwelling (including drains, gutters and external pipes); and

(b) keep in repair and proper working order the installations in the dwelling for:

- the supply of water, gas and electricity and for sanitation; and

- for space and water heating (s 11 of the Landlord and Tenant Act 1985).

This covenant cannot be excluded by agreement between the landlord and tenant, although there is a little used power for the parties to make a joint application to the court for an order varying or excluding it (s 15 of the Landlord and Tenant Act 1985).

A landlord only becomes liable under this covenant once he has been given notice of any works that need to be done to comply with it (*Al Hassani v Merrigan* [1988] 3 EGLR 88, CA). If the tenant is in breach of a repairing covenant, the landlord is entitled to damages. These damages may not exceed the amount by which the value of the landlord's reversionary interest has been reduced due to the breach (s 18(1) of the Landlord and Tenant Act 1927). The breach may also form a ground on which the court may order possession under Case 1 of Sched 15 to the Rent Act 1977 or Ground 12 of Sched 2 to the Housing Act 1988 (HA 1988).

There is also an implied obligation on the tenant not to commit acts of waste (damage or destruction). Breach of this will entitle the landlord to damages and potentially to possession under Case 3 or Ground 13.

Breach of a repairing covenant may also entitle a landlord to forfeiture of the lease during its contractual term. Before he can forfeit the lease, he must first serve a notice on all the tenants pursuant to s 146 of the Law of Property Act 1925, requiring the tenant to rectify the defect.

A tenant can bring an action against his landlord seeking specific performance of a repairing covenant (s 125 of the HA 1974). The tenant may also claim damages, the appropriate measure being the reduction in the value of the premises to him caused by the landlord's failure to repair. If the tenant carried out the repairs himself, then the amount so expended would represent the diminution in value. The tenant does not have the right to withhold rent because of a breach of repairing covenant by the landlord. However, a claim for even unliquidated damages arising out of such a breach can be treated as an equitable set off (*British Anzani (Felixstowe) Ltd v International Marine Management (UK) Ltd* [1980] QB 137). Even words in the lease requiring the tenant to pay the rent 'without any deductions' will not disentitle him from doing this (*Connaught Restaurants v Indoor Leisure* [1994] 4 All ER 834, CA). Therefore, a landlord will have very little remedy against a tenant who does withhold rent in such circumstances.

5.2 Gas regulations

The Gas Safety (Installation and Use) Regulations required landlords' compliance by 31 October 1995. Further regulations strengthened the impact of those provisions from 31 October 1996. Landlords have to take considerable steps to ensure the safety of their tenants where there are gas appliances owned by the landlord in the premises. The main duty on the landlord is the obvious one: not to install a gas appliance unless it can be used without constituting a danger to any person. Every year, the landlord must ensure that every gas appliance in the property is checked for safety by an approved person. This means, in effect, a member of the Council of Registered Gas Installers (CORGI). The landlord must also keep a record in respect of each gas appliance stating any defects identified and any remedial action that has been taken in respect of that defect. The landlord should keep some proof of each such inspection. An itemised receipt should be sufficient. Most CORGI engineers will be prepared, for a small additional charge, to issue a formal certificate of safety. This is probably only necessary for landlords who have a large number of properties and find difficulties keeping records or where there is a history of conflict with the tenants.

Any tenant who might be affected by a gas appliance is entitled to inspect the record which relates to it on giving the landlord reasonable notice. Landlords are under a duty to provide the tenant with a copy of the details of the inspection within 14 days of its being carried out, whether or not the tenant actually requests it. In the case of a new tenancy, the landlord will have to provide the tenant with a copy of the inspection record before the tenant moves in.

It is a defence for the landlord to show that he took all reasonable steps to comply with the Regulations, but was unable to do so. A landlord who employs a contractor to go to a property, notifies the tenants when the contractor is coming, and who isn't told by the tenants that the time is inconvenient, would probably have a defence if the contractor was not admitted by the tenants to the property.

A gas appliance for these purposes is one 'designed for use by a consumer of gas for heating, lighting, cooking, or other purposes'. This will includes boilers and other central heating devices as much as it does fires.

A failure to comply with these Regulations which resulted in a gas leak or explosion that caused the death of a tenant would probably lead to a manslaughter prosecution of the landlord. The penalties in such a case are likely to be infinitely more serious than can be imposed under the Regulations themselves.

5.3   Furniture regulations

The Furniture and Furnishings (Fire) (Safety) Regulations 1988 (SI 1988/1324, as amended by SI 1989/2358 and SI 1993/207) require landlords to comply with the same regulations as regards the provision of fire resistant furniture as currently apply to retailers. All furniture supplied under tenancies has to:

(a) have upholstery that complies with the 'cigarette test'. This is a test carried out according to a British Standard specification, designed to ensure that the furniture will not burst into flames when a cigarette is dropped on it. Beds, including mattresses and pillows, are exempt from this requirement;

(b) have a filling that complies with further 'ignitability tests';

(c) have any permanent covers that pass the 'match test'.

Furniture which satisfies these requirements will be labelled accordingly. Second hand shops and auctioneers should no longer sell furniture that does not comply with these Regulations.

5.4   Varying terms of the tenancy other than rent

When the contractual period of an assured tenancy expires, it will become a statutory periodic tenancy on the same terms as the contractual tenancy. However, within a year of expiry of the contractual term, either the landlord or the tenant may serve on the other a notice proposing a variation in the terms (s 6 of the HA 1988). This notice must be in the prescribed form (see 8.11). If the party on whom the notice is served does nothing, the proposed change will take effect after three months (s 6(3)(b) of the HA 1988). If he does wish to object, he may apply to a rent assessment committee for its adjudication. This must be done in the prescribed form (for information on which, see 8.12).

The committee, in determining whether to allow the proposed change, must have regard to whether or not those terms are ones which might reasonably be expected to be found in a tenancy of the property concerned (s 6(4) of the HA 1988). There is a discretion to vary the rent (upwards or downwards) to reflect the effect on the value of the tenancy resulting from any approved variation (s 6(5) of the HA 1988).

5.5   The tenant's right to quiet enjoyment

At common law, there is an implied term that the tenant is entitled to quiet enjoyment of the demised premises. The landlord is obliged not to do anything that will detract from the rights the tenant has been granted. The most serious breach of this covenant is wrongful eviction of the tenant. It is an offence for a landlord unlawfully to evict a residential occupier (whether or not a tenant) (s 1 of the Protection from Eviction Act 1977). If the tenant is unlawfully evicted, his first course if he wishes to return should be to seek an injunction compelling the landlord to re-admit him to the premises. The covenant to allow quiet enjoyment also applies so as to prohibit less drastic interferences with a tenant's rights. Such actions as cutting off services, deliberately allowing the premises to fall into a state of disrepair, and even forcing unwanted sexual attentions on a tenant, give the tenant a right to take action for breach of this covenant. (Though the mere withholding of normal 'social intercourse', even if that is to be expected by reason of the proximity in which the landlord and tenant live, cannot constitute a breach of this covenant: *Morris v Knight* (1999) CLY 3682.) The fact that the landlord was not motivated by a desire to force the tenant out does not affect the tenant's right to an injunction and/or damages, although the tenant would then be less likely to receive exemplary damages. An unlawful interference with a residential occupier's rights will usually constitute an offence under the Protection from Eviction Act 1977. The protection given to residential occupiers by the Protection from Eviction Act 1977 is somewhat reduced where the tenancy or licence is an excluded one under s 1(3A) of that Act (as inserted by s 29 of the HA 1988). This basically applies where the landlord is resident.

5.6   Damages for wrongful eviction at common law

At common law, an illegally evicted tenant is also entitled to damages, either in addition to or instead of an injunction. The normal measure of damages is the value of the loss of the tenancy. This may be a very considerable amount, especially in areas where there is a shortage of rented accommodation. The highest reported award (in fact against a solicitor whose negligence caused the loss of the tenancy) is £115,000, which was one-quarter of the value of the freehold (*Murray v Lloyd* [1989] 1 WLR 1060, Mummery J). If the eviction has been carried out in a particularly unpleasant manner, for instance violently, the tenant may be entitled to aggravated damages to compensate for the additional distress this has caused him. The court may also award exemplary damages where the landlord has been motivated by the belief that he would make a profit from his actions even after paying the tenant damages (*Drane v Evangelou* [1978] 1 WLR 455, CA).

5.7   Damages for wrongful eviction under the HA 1988

The HA 1988 introduced an elaborate scheme for the assessment of damages to be awarded to illegally evicted tenants. This scheme exists concurrently with the right to claim damages at common law for tort or breach of contract, though a tenant will not be able to recover damages on both bases in respect of a single claim (s 27(5) of the HA 1988). The Act provides that a residential occupier will be entitled to damages where he gives up his right to occupy the premises as a consequence of various specified acts done by his landlord with the intention of causing the occupier to give up the premises or refrain from exercising rights in respect of them (s 27). These acts include anything calculated to interfere with the peace or comfort of the occupier or his household or a persistent withdrawal or withholding of services reasonably required for the occupation of the premises (s 27(2)). The measure of damages to be awarded to an occupier who gives up the premises in those circumstances is the difference between the value of the landlord's interest in the building in which the premises are contained, with and without the occupier in occupation (s 28). In determining the value of the landlord's interest once the occupier is no longer present, it will be assumed that it is unlawful to redevelop the property (s 28(3)). However, if the occupier is reinstated in the premises before the commencement of proceedings, he will lose his right to damages under the Act (s 27(5)). Such an occupier may still have a valid claim at common law. However, s 27(5) would not seem to disentitle an occupier who commences proceedings for both an injunction and damages under the Act from recovering damages, even if he is reinstated by reason of obtaining the injunction before the hearing of the damages claim.

Damages under this section have been awarded against a landlord who, having obtained a possession order, enforced it himself, but without first obtaining a warrant from the court (*Haniff v Robinson* [1993] QB 419, CA). The highest reported award under this provision was £31,000 in *Tagro v Cafane* [1991] 1 WLR 378, CA.

5.8   Succession to protected and statutory tenancies under the RA 1977

When a protected or statutory tenant dies, the landlord is not always entitled to possession of the premises. If the spouse of the original tenant survives him and is living in the premises at the time of his death, she shall be entitled to remain in the premises as a statutory assured tenant (Sched 1, paras 1, 2 of the RA 1977). If there was no spouse, any other member of the tenant's family who had lived with him in the premises for the six months prior to his death may become the statutory assured tenant (Sched 1, para 3). If there is a dispute amongst various family members over who should become the statutory assured tenant, the matter should be referred to the county court by originating application. A person who succeeds to a statutory assured tenancy in this manner will be able to 'pass it on' when he dies, but at the death of the person to whom he passed it no further succession will generally be possible (Sched 1, paras 6, 7).

5.9   Succession to assured tenancies

The statutory right to succeed to a protected or statutory tenancy applies subject to certain modifications to assured tenancies (s 39 and Sched 4 to the HA 1988). A person who was living with the original tenant as 'husband and wife' shall be treated as his or her spouse (Sched 4, para 2(2) of the HA 1988). This expression can include a homosexual partner (*Sterling Housing Association v Fitzpatrick* [1999] 3 WLR 1113, HL). In the peculiar situation where more than one person was living with the deceased as a spouse, the court is given a power to determine which of them shall succeed to the tenancy (Sched 4, para 2(3)). The right to succeed is restricted to persons who lived with the tenant at the dwelling house for two years (Sched 4, para 3).

6 Recovering Possession

6.1 Introduction

Historically, residential tenants have had a considerable degree of protection from landlords who wished to regain possession of the demised property. The Rent Act (RA) 1977 perhaps represented the high point of the tenant's position in this respect. The protection was substantially eroded by the Housing Act (HA) 1988 and then by the amendments made by the HA 1996.

In any case, a landlord only has the right to evict where the contract between the tenant and himself purports to give him that right. This can be either because the agreed term of the tenancy has expired or because the landlord does not wish to renew a periodical tenancy. Alternatively, there may have been a breach of the terms of the tenancy which *prima facie* entitles the landlord to terminate it, usually under a forfeiture clause. The landlord's contractual right to evict is fettered in respect of periodic protected tenancies – though not the statutory continuation of a fixed term tenancy after that term has expired – under the RA 1977 by the requirement that he must first serve a notice to quit in the prescribed form (see 8.7) at least 28 days before it is due to take effect. The HA 1988 provides for the service of a notice of intention of seeking possession before the landlord becomes entitled to evict a tenant.

Even where the contractual right to evict has arisen and the appropriate notice served the landlord can exercise that right only if one of the conditions specified by the RA 1977 or the HA 1988 has also arisen, though after six months of an assured shorthold tenancy, as most tenancies granted on after 28 February 1997 will be, the right to possession effectively becomes automatic. All but two of the conditions under the 1977 Act are contained in Pts I and II of Sched 15 to the Act and are referred to as 'Cases'. Except for the special provision in respect of assured shorthold tenancies, the conditions under the 1988 Act are contained in Sched 2 to that Act and are referred to as 'Grounds'. Where the agreement under which the tenant occupies the property is neither a protected, nor a statutory, nor an assured tenancy, the rights of the tenant are, of course, much less extensive. Even then, however, the landlord is not able to enforce his contractual right unfettered and, in particular, he may not evict the tenant without first obtaining a court order.

6.2 The circumstances in which possession may be recovered against a protected or statutory tenant under the RA 1977

The circumstances are specified in ss 98 and 101, and Pts I and II of Sched 15 to the Rent Acts. If the circumstances specified in s 98 and Cases 1–6 and 8–10 (Case 7 has been repealed) arise, the court has a discretion to grant possession if it considers it reasonable to do so. Where the circumstances specified in s 101 and Cases 11–20 arise, the court must make a possession order.

6.2.1 Case 1: non-payment of rent or breach of other term of tenancy

This Case applies where any rent due from the tenant has not been paid or the tenant has been in breach of any other legally enforceable term of the tenancy. Courts are normally reluctant to order possession on the grounds of arrears of rent alone if there is any realistic prospect of the arrears being paid off. A common course is to make a possession order and suspend it for so long as a prescribed amount of the arrears and all future payments are regularly made. Where arrears of rent are alleged, proceedings must be begun in the prescribed form (see 8.15).

Where there is a forefeiture clause and the tenant's default, for instance going bankrupt, brings that clause into operation, that will be treated as a breach of the terms of the tenancy for the purposes of this case. It does not matter that going bankrupt was not specifically otherwise prohibited by the tenancy agreement (*Cadogan Estates v MacMahon* [2000] 4 All ER 897, HL).

6.2.2 Case 2: nuisance or illegal use of premises

This Case applies where the tenant, anyone residing with him or a sub-tenant has been guilty of a nuisance or causing annoyance to adjoining occupiers or has been convicted of using or allowing the dwelling to be used for immoral or illegal purposes.

6.2.3 Case 3: waste

This Case applies where the condition of the dwelling has deteriorated due to acts of waste (neglect) by the tenant or anyone living with him. The Case will also apply if such acts have been committed by anyone who is a lodger or a sub-tenant, but only if the tenant has not taken reasonable steps to remove that person.

6.2.4 Case 4: deterioration of furniture

This provision is the same, *mutatis mutandis*, as Case 3 where the condition of the furniture in the premises has deteriorated due to ill-treatment.

6.2.5 Case 5: tenant's notice to quit

This Case applies where the tenant has given notice to quit and, in consequence, the landlord has taken steps that would result in him being seriously prejudiced were possession not granted. This Case is rarely relied upon, but it is hard to see a court refusing possession if the landlord had entered into an unconditional contract to sell or relet the premises in reliance on a tenant's intention to go.

6.2.6 Case 6: sub-letting by tenant

This Case applies where the tenant has, without the consent of the landlord, sub-let or assigned the whole of the dwelling.

6.2.7 Case 8: employees' accommodation

This Case applies where the tenant was let into possession of the dwelling as a term of his employment with the landlord or a former landlord and that employment has ceased. To take advantage of this Case, the landlord must also establish that he now requires the premises as a dwelling for someone engaged in his full time employment. This Case does not apply to agricultural employees.

6.2.8 Case 9: property required by landlord

This Case applies where the dwelling is reasonably required by the landlord as a residence for himself, his children who are over 18, his parents or his parents-in-law. This does not apply if the landlord became such by purchasing the property unless the purchase was before a date specified in the Case, the latest of which is 24 May 1974. (Becoming landlord by purchase must be distinguished from purchasing the property and then becoming landlord, which does not prevent this Case applying.)

6.2.9 Case 10: overcharging sub-tenants

This Case applies where the tenant sub-lets all or part of the premises at a rent which is in excess of the registered fair or reasonable rent (if any and as appropriate) for that part of the premises.

6.2.10   Case 11: owner-occupiers

For Case 11 to apply, certain conditions have to have been satisfied before the tenancy is granted. If these have been satisfied the landlord will be entitled to possession on the basis of one of the reasons laid down in Pt V of Sched 15 to the RA 1977. These are where:

(a) the dwelling is required as residence for the landlord or any member of his family who resided with him when he last occupied the dwelling as a residence;

(b) the landlord has died and the dwelling is required as a residence for a member of his family who resided with him at the time of his death;

(c) the landlord has died and the dwelling is required by a successor in title as a residence or for the purpose of selling it with vacant possession;

(d) the dwelling is subject to a mortgage made by deed before the granting of the tenancy, and the mortgagee is entitled to exercise a power of sale and requires the dwelling in order to dispose of it with vacant possession pursuant to that power; and

(e) the landlord wishes to dispose of the property with vacant possession and use the proceeds to buy a residence which is suitable for his needs having regard to his place of work, which the dwelling let is not. (Condition (2) (see 6.2.11) does not apply to Case 11.)

6.2.11   Case 12: retirement homes

For Case 12 to apply, certain conditions have to have been satisfied before the tenancy is granted. If these have been satisfied, the landlord will be entitled to possession on the basis of one of the reasons specified in Pt V of Sched 15 to the RA 1977. These are:

(a) Condition (2): '... the landlord has retired from regular employment and requires the dwelling as a residence'; and

(b) Conditions (3), (4) and (5) as listed above, 6.2.10.

6.2.12   Cases 13, 14, 15, 16, 17, 18 and 19

For explanations of Cases 13–19, see 2.7.3, 2.7.4, 2.7.5, 2.7.6 and 2.7.7. Once the condition that has to be satisfied on the tenancy's grant has been satisfied, the landlord will be entitled to possession on the occurrence of the event specified in the appropriate Case.

6.2.13   Case 20: homes owned by members of the armed forces

For Case 20 to apply, certain conditions have to have been satisfied before the tenancy is granted. If these have been satisfied, the landlord will be entitled to possession on the basis of one of the reasons specified in Pt V of Sched 15 to the RA 1977. These are conditions (3), (4), (5) and (6), which are set out in 6.2.10.

6.2.14   Suitable alternative accommodation: s 98

A court may make a possession order if it is satisfied that suitable alternative accommodation is available for the tenant, or will be when the possession order takes effect. This alternative accommodation may be, but does not need to be, provided by the landlord. Rules about what may constitute suitable alternative accommodation are set out in Pt IV of Sched 15. A certificate from a local authority that it will provide suitable alternative accommodation will be conclusive on that question (para (3)). However, even once accommodation is found to be suitable, whether because of the authority's certificate or otherwise, the court still has a discretion whether or not to order possession.

6.2.15   Overcrowded dwellings: s 101

Where a dwelling is overcrowded, the provisions which prevent a landlord from recovering possession are suspended. 'Overcrowded' is defined in Pt X of the HA 1985. A dwelling will be overcrowded if there are not sufficient rooms for every occupant over the age of 10 not to have to share a bedroom with someone of the opposite sex unless they are living with that person as husband and wife (s 325 of the HA 1985). There are also minimum permissible sizes for the rooms people occupy (s 326). The material date for the purposes of this section is the date of trial, so if occupants have left the dwelling between the commencement of proceedings and trial, resulting in it no longer being overcrowded, the tenant will be entitled to the usual statutory protection. The fact that a landlord is in breach of his covenant by allowing the premises to become overcrowded will not defeat a possession claim brought under this section (*Buswell v Goodwin* [1971] 1 WLR 92, CA).

6.3   Procedure for obtaining possession against a protected tenant

The summary procedure for obtaining possession against tenants on the basis of Cases 11–20 did not survive the CPR 1998. However, in cases where there is unlikely to be a substantial dispute of fact, the procedure provided for by Pt 8 of the CPR will be appropriate. This involves commencing an action without particulars of claim, but serving all the supporting written evidence along with the claim form. The defendant then has 14 days to serve an acknowledgment of service, stating whether or not he contests the claim, along with any written evidence upon which he wishes to rely. The defendant may object to the use of the Part 7 procedure if he alleges that there actually is a substantial question of fact to be determined, and if he indicates such an objection, the court will give directions. If the procedure is continued with, a final hearing will generally be obtained more quickly than if the Part 7 procedure is used.

In other situations, the more general jurisdiction under Pt 7 of the CPR should be invoked. Such action may be commenced only after the notice to quit has expired, as no right to possession exists before that time, though no notice needs to be served if there is a statutory tenancy. If possession is claimed wholly or partly on the basis of rent arrears, the prescribed form N119 must be used (see 6.12).

Service is normally effected by the court posting the summons to the defendant. If, for some reason, the claimant believes that this method will not bring the summons to the defendant's attention, he may request that the court serve it by a bailiff. Alternatively, he may take the summons and attempt to serve the summons himself or by his solicitors. If the latter course is adopted, a certificate of service will be necessary if the defendant does not attend the hearing.

6.4   Summary procedure for obtaining possession against licensees and squatters

This is provided for by CCR Ord 24 and RSC Ord 113, which have survived the CPR. The procedure is available to a person claiming possession of land which he alleges is occupied solely by a person or persons (not being a tenant or tenants holding over after the termination of the tenancy) who entered into or remained in occupation without his licence or consent or that of any predecessor in title of his (CCR Ord 24 r 1; RSC Ord 113 r 1).

The order is intended primarily as a device for evicting squatters, but there is no reason why it cannot be used against an unwanted lodger who has no contractual right to remain. The courts are reluctant to allow this procedure to be used against long standing licensees (*Bristol Corporation v Persons Unknown* [1974] 1 WLR 365, Pennycuick VC) and people who have an arguable claim to be tenants (*Cudworth v Masefield* (1984) *The Times*, 16 May, DC). If the defence advanced is totally disbelieved by the judge, summary judgment may be entered even if it does raise a triable issue (*Filemart v Avery* [1989] 46 EG 92, CA). If a landlord fails in a claim under the summary procedure, he is entitled to commence a possession action in the normal way.

The applicant must make an application using a CPR Part 8 claim form, filing a witness statement or affidavit in support. The Part 8 form is effectively the old form N312 with a statement of truth added (see CPR PD 8B Section B and CPR PD 4 Table 3). The witness statement must state the applicant's interest in the land; the circumstances in which land has been occupied without his licence or consent and in which his claim to possession arises; and that he does not know the name of any person occupying the land who is not named in the application (CCR Ord 24 r 2; RSC Ord 113 r 3) (see 8.16 and 8.17 for a sample Part 8 claim form and witness statement respectively).

Service can be effected personally, by an officer of the court leaving the documents at the premises, on the respondent's solicitor, if he will accept service, or in such other manner as the court may direct (CCR Ord 24 r 3(1); RSC Ord 113 r 4(1)). In addition to such service, the applicant must, unless the court directs otherwise, attach copies of the documents to the main door or other conspicuous part of the premises and, if practical, insert them through the letter box addressed to 'The occupants' (CCR Ord 24 r 3(2); RSC Ord 113 r 4(2)). The application will be heard not less than five days (two days in the case of non-residential premises) after the day of service (CCR Ord 24 r 5(1); RSC Ord 113 r 6(1)). The hearing may be expedited with the leave of the court in the case of urgency. There is no provision for making a monetary claim under this order. Some practitioners believe that the High Court procedure is quicker and more effective. In deciding in which court to commence proceedings, it should be borne in mind that costs are rarely recovered against occupiers evicted in such circumstances.

6.5 The circumstances in which possession may be obtained against an assured tenant under the HA 1988

There were 16 'Grounds' for possession specified in the HA 1988, the first eight of which are mandatory. Two more discretionary Grounds were added by the HA 1996. They are listed in Sched 2 to the Act. 'Grounds' to all intents and purposes has the same meaning as 'Cases' does under the RA 1977. In addition, there is a special provision contained in s 20 of the 1988 Act for terminating assured shorthold tenancies.

6.5.1 Ground 1: landlord has resided or wishes to reside in the property

Ground 1 applies where the landlord has occupied the property as his principal or only home and/or now requires it for himself or his spouse as their only or principal home. A landlord who has bought the property during the current tenancy is not entitled to rely on this Ground. There are no restrictions relating to the reasons for which a landlord who has resided there previously now requires possession. The landlord should have served notice of his intention to recover possession under this Case when the tenancy was originally granted. The notice requirement can be dispensed with if the court considers it just and equitable to do so. A landlord who has not resided there previously will merely have to prove that he requires the property as his or his spouse's only or principal home.

6.5.2 Ground 2: possession required by mortgagee

Ground 2 applies where a mortgagee under a mortgage of the property which was granted before the tenancy wishes to claim possession to enable him to exercise a power of sale conferred on him either by the mortgage or by s 101 of the Law of Property Act 1925. Again, there is a requirement either that the tenant was given notice of the possibility of possession being obtained under this Ground or that the court thinks it just and equitable to dispense with the notice requirement.

6.5.3 Grounds 3, 4 and 5: lettings of holiday accommodation, lettings by educational establishments and lettings of property intended for ministers of religion

Grounds 3, 4 and 5 are similar to Cases 13, 14 and 15 respectively (see 2.7.3, 2.7.4 and 2.7.5). They apply to out-of-season holiday lets, lettings by recognised educational institutions and lettings of property intended for and now required by ministers of religion. In respect of Grounds 3 and 4, the landlord does not have to show anything other than that the appropriate notice was correctly and justifiably served before the tenancy commenced. In respect of Ground 5, it is also necessary to show that the property is now required for occupation by a minister of religion.

6.5.4 Ground 6: demolition or reconstruction of premises

Ground 6 applies where the landlord intends to carry out substantial work on the property, including demolition or reconstruction, which it is not practicable to do with the tenant *in situ*. This Ground is not available where the landlord (or, if there are joint landlords, any of them) bought his interest during the currency of the present tenancy. If the tenant is willing to agree to a variation of the terms of his tenancy, including accepting a tenancy of just part of the property, so as to allow the work to be carried out, the landlord will not be entitled to possession. This provision seems for the most part to be designed to give landlords a lever to persuade tenants to agree to redevelopment, rather than actually lead to possession orders. If possession is ordered pursuant to this section, the court will order the landlord to pay a sum equal to the tenant's reasonable removal expenses (s 11 of the HA 1988).

6.5.5 Ground 7: tenancy passing by will or intestacy

Ground 7 applies where the periodic tenancy has passed by will or intestacy on the death of the former tenant. It is the actual commencement of proceedings, not the service of a s 8 notice, that is relevant for this purpose (*Shepping v Osada* [2000] 2 EGLR 38, CA). The landlord can commence proceedings under this Ground in the 12 months thereafter. If he did not know of the former tenant's death at the time it occurred, the 12 month period may, in the court's discretion, start to run from when he found out about it. The Ground expressly declares that the acceptance of rent by the landlord after the former tenant's death does not create a new tenancy. This merely states the position at common law, but nonetheless removes an issue which seems to cause many practitioners much unnecessary worry. This Ground applies only where the tenancy has passed by will or on intestacy, rather than under the statutory succession provisions.

6.5.6 Ground 8: two or three months' arrears of rent

Ground 8 applies where the landlord commences proceedings on the basis that two months' rent (in the case of monthly tenants), or eight weeks (in the case of a tenancy where rent is paid weekly or fortnightly) is in arrears. If rent is paid quarterly or yearly, at least one quarter's rent must be more than three months in arrears. These arrears must exist both at the time when the notice under s 8 of the HA 1988 (see 6.7) is served and at the date of the hearing. The provision seems to make no allowance for the situation when arrears have accrued due to no fault of the tenant's, perhaps through the failure of a local authority to pay housing benefit. Theoretically, this Ground could apply even if the arrears have accrued due to the landlord deliberately avoiding receipt of payment. In those circumstances, the rules of equity may protect the tenant. In *Bessa Plus plc v Lancaster* [1997] EGCS 42, the Court of Appeal held that the landlord was entitled to possession after rejecting payments from the tenant's cohabitee. This decision was made on the basis that she had not tendered the payment as the tenant's agent, and thus suggests that, had she been acting as his agent or had the payment come directly from him and then been rejected, possession would not have been ordered pursuant to this Ground. Courts tend, in practice, also to avoid the harshness of this Ground by adjourning possession claims brought under it to establish the housing benefit position. In the period before the adjourned hearing, pressure can be brought to bear on the local authority, if necessary by the issuing of witness summonses against its officers, to meet its obligations.

6.5.7 Ground 9: suitable alternative accommodation available

This Ground, which is the first of the discretionary grounds, applies where suitable alternative accommodation is available for the tenant. This is analogous to the provision in s 98(1)(a) of the RA 1977 (see 6.2.14). 'Suitable alternative accommodation' is defined in Pt III of Sched 2. Where a local housing authority has certified that such accommodation will be available to the tenant, that will be conclusive (Sched 2, Pt III, para 3(2)). Otherwise, the court will have to decide whether the property is suitable for the tenant, having regard to the needs of the tenant and his family and proximity to place of work. The property must also either be similar to that provided by local housing associations for people in similar circumstances to the tenant, or be reasonably suitable for the tenant and his family having regard to extent and character (para 3(1)). If there is a furnished tenancy, the furniture provided in the alternative accommodation must also be similar if the accommodation is to be deemed suitable. Although the schedule expresses itself as defining the concept of suitable alternative accommodation, in most cases it will have left open the factual question of suitability for the court to decide. Where the court makes an order for possession pursuant to this Ground (or Ground 6), it will order the landlord to pay the tenant a sum equal to his reasonable expenses likely to be incurred in moving (s 11 of the HA 1988).

6.5.8 Ground 10: rent arrears

Ground 10 applies where there are some arrears of rent, both when proceedings are begun and when the notice of intention to commence proceedings (see 6.7) was served on the tenant. In practice, this Ground will usually overlap with Grounds 8 and 11.

6.5.9 Ground 11: persistent delay in paying rent

Ground 11 applies where 'the tenant has persistently delayed paying rent that has become lawfully due'. The draftsman seems to have deliberately left open the question of when exactly a landlord will be able to rely on this Ground. On a strict reading, the reason for the non-payment will be irrelevant: all that matters is whether or not it has occurred persistently. In practice, the courts take a broader view of the provision.

6.5.10   Ground 12: breach of terms of the tenancy

Ground 12 applies where the tenant has been in breach of a term of the tenancy other than payment of rent. This has similar effect to the part of Case 1 which relates to terms other than payment of rent (see 6.2.1).

6.5.11   Grounds 13, 14 and 15: waste, nuisance or illegal use of premises and deterioration of furniture

Grounds 13, 14 and 15 are similar respectively to Cases 3, 2 and 4 (see 6.2.3, 6.2.2 and 6.2.4). They apply where the tenant has caused the condition of the dwelling house to deteriorate; where the tenant has been guilty of conduct which is a nuisance to adjoining occupiers; and where the tenant has caused damage to furniture provided under the tenancy. The only substantive variation is that damage to the common parts is included in Ground 13, whereas Case 3 is confined to the dwelling house itself. A wider Ground 14 applies since the passing of the HA 1996, where the misbehaviour of the tenant or anyone else residing in, or visiting, the dwelling house causes nuisance to anyone residing in, or carrying on a lawful activity in the locality of, the dwelling. The court, in considering whether to make an order, should have regard to local public opinion on the matter. In *West Kent Housing Association v Davies* (1999) 31 HLR 415, the Court of Appeal reversed a judge's decision not to make an order despite finding that the tenant had caused a nuisance by repairing old cars at the premises and been racially abusive and threatening to neighbours. This Ground will also apply if an arrestable offence is committed in, or in the locality of, the dwelling house. The primary motivation behind this provision seems to be to enable landlords to evict drug dealers, though it can also be used against handlers of stolen goods. It might also be a useful device for a landlord facing pressure from neighbours to evict someone convicted of sexual offences, so long as the offences have actually taken place at the demised premises.

6.5.12   Ground 16: employee tenants

Ground 16 applies where the letting was in consequence of the tenant's employment by the landlord and that employment has ceased. A claim on this basis need not be adjourned because the tenant has made an application to the employment tribunal seeking reinstatement (*Whitbread West Pennines Ltd v Reedy* [1988] ICR 807, CA).

6.5.13   Ground 17: tenancy obtained by a false statement

Ground 17 will apply if the tenant or anyone acting on his behalf obtained the tenancy by recklessly or knowingly making a false statement. It is most likely to be used where something is done to conceal the true identity of the tenant from the landlord.

6.5.14   Ground 14A: domestic violence

Ground 14A applies after the HA 1996 comes into force. It will only apply where the landlord is a registered social landlord or charitable housing trust. If one partner has been forced out by the other's violence, possession may then be obtained against the remaining partner, regardless of who was the original tenant, but only if the court is satisfied that the non-violent partner is unlikely to return.

6.6   Obtaining possession against an assured shorthold tenant

Once both the term of the assured shorthold tenancy and six months have expired, the tenant can have no defence to a claim for possession so long as the landlord has followed the correct procedure. A notice must be served by the landlord giving the tenant two months' written notice that he requires possession of the property. This notice can be given during the currency of the tenancy, ideally (from the landlord's point of view) expiring on the same day as the tenancy terminates or the notice to quit takes effect (s 21(2) of the HA 1988). If the landlord takes no action on the expiry of the term, the tenancy continues, but he will remain able to serve the two months' notice at any time.

6.7   Procedure for recovering possession against an assured tenant

Section 8 of the HA 1988 requires the landlord to give the tenant notice that he intends taking proceedings before doing so. The tenant must be given notice that the landlord intends to start possession proceedings and the Ground(s) to be relied upon must be specified (for the prescribed form of notice, see 8.1). Only two weeks' notice need be given unless one or more of Grounds 1, 2, 5–7, 9 and 16 is relied upon, when the period is two months. Since the coming into force of the HA 1996, proceedings can be commenced as soon as the notice is served if Ground 14 (nuisance) is relied upon (s 8(4) of the HA 1988). The court, however, has a discretion to dispense with this notice if it considers it just and equitable to do so unless possession is sought in reliance on Ground 8 (rent more than two or three months in arrears) (s 8(1)(b) of the HA 1988).

After expiry of the notice (or before, if the court is to be asked to dispense with notice), proceedings should be commenced following the same procedure as is used for recovering possession against a protected or statutory tenant (see 6.3) unless the summary procedure can be invoked (see 6.8). Section 9 of the HA 1988 gives the court discretion to adjourn proceedings where possession is sought pursuant to one of the discretionary Grounds, but if it does so, it is required to impose terms with regard to payment of rent and arrears, unless doing so would cause the tenant exceptional hardship.

The notice need not set out the statutory Ground verbatim, though in practice it would be advisable to do so. A notice claiming possession on the basis of Ground 8 was held invalid because of the omission of words to the effect that that Ground only applied if there had been the requisite arrears both at the date of the notice and the date of the hearing (*Mountain v Hastings* [1993] 25 HLR 427).

6.8   The summary procedure under the HA 1988

If the tenancy was subject to a notice served pursuant to Grounds 1, 3, 4 or 5 of Sched 2 to the HA 1988 or it was an assured shorthold tenancy (see 2.6) which has come to an end, the landlord may use the accelerated procedure to obtain possession. The procedure is contained in CCR Ord 49 rr 6 and 6A, introduced from 1 November 1993 and retained by the CPR. This procedure is not available to a mortgagee claiming under Ground 2 (r 6(3)(b)). Nor is the procedure available where the landlord is asking the court to dispense with service of a notice, whether one that should have been served before the tenancy was granted or the notice of intention of seeking possession that is usually a prerequisite to a possession claim (rr 6(3) and 6A(3)). However, in straightforward cases, where all the formalities have been complied with, it should make obtaining possession a relatively simple task. The procedure will only lead to possession. If the landlord is seeking rent arrears or other relief, he will have to do so by way of a separate action.

The form, N5B, takes the form of an affidavit and, as such, has to be sworn by the landlord. All relevant notices have to be exhibited to the form.

Once the form is submitted, the tenant has 14 days to respond. If no reply is received, the landlord can then request the court to make the possession order (rr 6(12) and 6A(14)).

If the tenant does reply, the papers will be given to a judge. If the judge believes that the reply raises an issue that should lead to a trial – and the reasons why it might are listed in the Order – he will order there to be a hearing (r 6(14) and r 6A(16)). The making of summary possession orders in this way, without giving the tenant a meaningful opportunity to be heard, could well be the subject of challenge under the right to a fair trial provided for in the Human Rights Act 1998 after that Act comes into force. If there is nothing of substance in the notice, he will order possession (r 6(15) and r 6A(17)). The judge may also order a hearing of his own motion if he is not satisfied that the application does entitle the landlord to possession.

6.9   The notice to quit

A protected periodic tenancy of a dwelling house, subject to the RA 1977, can generally only be terminated (by landlord or tenant) by the service of a valid notice to quit. No notice is necessary to terminate a statutory tenancy, and the requirement for a notice to quit has been supplanted by the 's 8' notice necessary to end an assured tenancy (see 6.8). Where the notice is given by the landlord, it is valid only if in writing, given not less than four weeks before it is due to take effect and containing prescribed information on the tenant's rights (s 5 of the Protection from Eviction Act 1977). A notice given on the same day of the week as that on which it is to expire four weeks later is valid (*Schnabel v Allard* [1967] 1 QB 627, CA). The notice must also comply with common law rules and be of at least the same length as the period of the tenancy, so if there is a monthly tenancy it must give one month's notice rather than 28 days. Further, it must expire either on the last day of one tenancy period or on the first day of the next. The notice can be served in any of the usual ways: personally, by leaving it at the premises so that it will come to the tenant's attention, or by post. Service on one joint tenant will constitute service on all of them, but it would be unwise not to serve them all individually, in case difficulties arose in proving that a particular one of them had been served.

The rules concerning notices to quit also apply where there is a periodic licence agreement, whether or not the agreement constitutes a restricted contract and whether it was granted before or after the coming into force of the HA 1988 (s 5(1A) of the Protection from

Eviction Act 1977). However, the rules concerning notices to quit do not apply at all if there is an 'excluded' licence or tenancy. Such an agreement is one entered into on or after 15 January 1990 where the tenant or licensee has the use of any part of the accommodation in common with the landlord or licensor or any member of his family (s 3(2A) of the Protection from Eviction Act 1977). For an excluded tenancy or licence to exist, the landlord, licensor or member of his family must have been residing in the accommodation both at the commencement of the tenancy or licence and at the time when it is sought to end it.

6.10 Claiming possession against a lessee under a restricted contract

There is very little restraint on the circumstances in which the court will grant possession to the holder of the lessor's interest under a restricted contract which commenced after 29 November 1980 once the term of that contract has expired (see above, Chapter 2). However, the court does have a discretion to postpone the coming into force of such an order for a period of up to three months (s 106A(2), (3) of the RA 1977).

6.11 Basic points on pleading in possession actions

It is almost always proper and advantageous to commence a possession action in the county court. The county courts are far more familiar with such claims, and the procedure is quicker (see 6.1.1). The fact that the property is subject to the RA 1977 or the HA 1988 should be specifically pleaded. If a notice to quit has to be served (see 6.9), it is vital that proceedings are not commenced until it has expired. No right exists to possession until that time and the court will not allow amendment to incorporate a subsequently arising right into the claim. If a notice of intention of bringing proceedings has been served, the landlord should wait until that has expired unless he is confident that he can persuade the court to dispense with the requirement of notice (see 6.7).

Where the landlord is claiming possession on a basis that includes arrears of rent, he must use the prescribed form of particulars of claim (see 6.12). If the landlord wishes to assert that there is a licence, but fears that the court may find a tenancy exists, it is quite acceptable to plead the licence, but with the landlord's remedies against a tenant in the alternative (see 2.1). The way in which the tenancy has been terminated should be specifically pleaded, as should the grounds on which possession is sought. It is quite acceptable to plead more than one RA 1977 Case or HA 1988 Ground. If there is a claim for a money sum, interest should be pleaded in the body of the pleading as well as the prayer (s 69 of the County Courts Act 1984).

6.12 Claiming possession where there are arrears of rent

In November 1993, CCR Ord 6 r 3(3) was amended to introduce a prescribed form on which all claims for possession of dwelling houses based on rent arrears must be commenced, a provision which has survived the CPR. This applies to mortgage arrears cases as well as landlord and tenant matters. It requires information, for instance, about the tenant's finances, that would not be appropriate in traditional proceedings. If this form is not used, the court may allow the claimant to amend the particulars to incorporate the form or may strike them out altogether. The form is set out below, 8.15.

6.13 Court procedures generally

Many of the specific procedures to be used in residential tenancy cases will override the general provisions of the CPR. However, once proceedings have been contested, the requirements for the parties to complete allocation questionnaires and then for the matter to be allocated to a 'track' will apply (CPR 26). Claims for money where the amount in issue is less than £5,000 will normally be allocated to the small claims track. However, if there is a claim against a landlord for damages for harassment or unlawful eviction, it cannot be allocated to this track (CPR 26.7) The main effect of allocation to the small claims track is that *inter partes* costs, other than court fees and witness' expenses, are not usually ordered. Most residential tenancy cases, except where there is a claim for more than £15,000 or an exceptionally complex issue, will be allocated to the fast track. This enables costs to be awarded, but on a lower scale, particularly for those incurred at trial, than those which are allocated to the strangely named 'multi-track', for the most serious cases.

7 Jurisdiction, Legal Aid, Costs and Court Fees

7.1 Courts' jurisdiction

Claims relating to residential tenancies should almost invariably be brought in the county court. Proceedings for possession may only be commenced in the court for the district in which the land is situated (CCR Ord 4 r 3, which has survived the CPR).

7.1.1 Jurisdiction and costs

The rules relating to costs as they concern actions brought under the Rent Act 1977 (RA 1977) and the Housing Act 1988 (HA 1988) are designed to encourage parties to bring their claims in the county court rather than the High Court. Most significantly, if certain actions are brought in the High Court, the party who brought that action will not be able to recover any costs if he succeeds. (If he does not succeed, costs may be awarded against him on the usual basis.) These actions are listed in s 141(5) of the RA 1977 and include under that Act:

(a) actions to recover excess rent paid to a landlord;

(b) possession actions except those where the court has no discretion after the ground for ordering possession has been established; and

(c) actions to recover illegal premiums paid under or for a protected tenancy.

If a claim is brought in the High Court in respect of a matter relating to a post-HA 1988 tenancy which could be brought in the county court, the claimant will be able to recover only as much costs as he would in the county court (s 40(4) of the HA 1988). If a money claim is brought in the High Court which should have been brought in the county court, costs awarded to the claimant may be reduced by up to 25% (s 51 of the Supreme Court Act 1981). It is hard to envisage any circumstances where that provision would not apply to a possession action if it were commenced in the High Court.

7.2   Legal aid

Frequently, a party to an action arising out of residential premises will be entitled to public funding under the Access to Justice Act 1999. (Although the term 'legal aid' may be technically obsolete, it is still far more widely used by practitioners, judges, the public and the media than the various derivatives of 'public funding', and will be retained in this text.) Eligibility for legal aid is dependent on satisfying the Legal Services Commission (as the Legal Aid Board has become) that the nature of the prospective assisted person's case is such as to merit its grant and that he has disposal income and capital that are below certain levels. If legal aid is granted, the assisted person may be required to pay a contribution depending on his financial resources. This contribution is paid to the Legal Services Commission, and its payment or non-payment does not affect the solicitor's remuneration. The Legal Services Commission has a charge on any money or other property which is recovered or retained by the assisted person as a result of the proceedings in which he is legally aided. This charge is up to the extent of the assisted person's actual costs, less any contribution paid by him and any costs recovered from the other side. This charge is subject to certain exemptions.

7.2.1 Legal aid and tenants

If the applicant for legal aid is a defendant tenant who has some reasonable prospect of successfully defending the action or persuading the court to postpone a possession order, then legal aid will probably be granted, subject to him being financially eligible. In cases where the solicitor is first consulted just before the hearing of a possession claim, it may be possible to obtain emergency legal aid. In cases of real and immediate urgency, this can be done by telephoning the local area office of the Legal Services Commission. Otherwise, the application should be made in writing. An alternative to making an application for emergency legal aid is to ask the court for an adjournment whilst the full application is considered. This can be done by writing to the other side seeking their agreement to this course. If they do not agree, the applicant should be sent along to court with a letter explaining the position and pointing out that a request was made of the other side beforehand. Where possession is sought against a tenant, it is usually to the tenant's advantage to obtain an adjournment as he will, of course, be able to remain in possession until after the eventual hearing. For this reason, the court may sometimes be reluctant to order an adjournment if the only reason is the fact that a legal aid application is pending. If the tenant has a meritorious defence, this should be explained in the letter. The court is much more likely to agree to an adjournment on that basis than if it is merely a case where the tenant wishes to be represented when asking the court to exercise its discretion not to evict him.

7.2.2 Legal aid and landlords

Landlords are potentially entitled to legal aid, but are far less likely to be granted it, because generally, their financial resources will make them ineligible. However, property that is the subject matter of the dispute will usually be disregarded. In any case, in computing capital, the value of the applicant's main or only dwelling is disregarded. A resident landlord therefore might still qualify for legal aid notwithstanding his ownership of the property in question.

7.3 Costs

At the conclusion of a case, the general rule is that the unsuccessful party will be ordered to pay the successful party's legal costs. Where possession is sought against a tenant, but the court only makes a suspended order, the landlord will be considered the successful party. Generally, if a claim for rent arrears or damages only succeeds in part, the claimant will be taken to be the successful party for the purpose of costs. The amount of costs allowed is normally assessed on the standard basis, though if the behaviour of either party has been such as to merit it, or a properly made offer of settlement has been declined, but not beaten at trial, indemnity costs may be awarded. The standard basis allows for costs that are 'proportionate to the matters in issue' with any doubts as to reasonableness or proportionality being resolved in favour of the paying party (CPR 44.4(2)). If the indemnity basis applies, costs will be allowed regardless of proportionality, but those that are unreasonably incurred or unreasonable in amount will be disallowed (CPR 44.4(1)).

In cases allocated to the fast track (see 6.13), which most contested possession and many rent actions will be, this rather vague formula is supplemented by the specific scales of costs.

7.3.1 Assessment of costs

Since the introduction of the CPR, costs are most frequently summarily assessed at the end of the application or trial. A costs estimate should be filed and served on the other side at least 24 hours before the hearing (CPR PD 43). This should specify:

(a) the number of hours claimed;

(b) the hourly rate claimed;

(c) the grade of fee earner (partner or other experienced solicitor, solicitor of less than four years' admission, legal executive or trainee);

(d) the amount and nature of disbursements claimed;

(e) solicitor's costs for attending the hearing;

(f) counsel's fees;

(g) VAT.

Legally aided parties are not required to serve such an estimate and summary assessments will not be made of their costs. However, where a costs order is made against a legally aided party, the amount should be summarily assessed, even if an order is made that the costs order not be enforced (see 7.3.2).

At the conclusion of the hearing, the judge will first consider whether to make a costs order at all. Once that is done, a decision will be made as to amount. If the hearing lasts for more than a day, or there has been a multi-track trial, the judge will normally order a detailed assessment. It is no longer necessary for the judge to certify that a hearing is fit for counsel. Many courts have indicated that the judges will consider indicating, in a suitable case, either of their own motion or on the application of the paying party, that counsel's attendance was not necessary or appropriate. Where a party is represented by more than one counsel, certification is still necessary.

7.3.2 Recovering costs against a legally aided opponent

Where an assisted person is the loser, the court can only make an order for costs to be recovered against him after having had regard to all the circumstances, including the means of the parties and their conduct in relation to the case (s 11 of the Access to Justice Act 1999). The usual practice is for the court to make an award on the usual *inter partes* principles and then order that some or all of it not be enforced without leave of the court. Sometimes, the sum immediately enforceable will be an amount equivalent to the contribution the assisted person had to pay towards his own legal aid. If there were a nil contribution, then it is likely that no part of the order against the assisted person would be enforceable. If the assisted person's circumstances improve during the subsequent six years, then an application can be made to the court to enforce the award. Although this was traditionally referred to as the 'football pools order', changes in gambling fashion mean that names associated with the National Lottery are more likely to be used in future.

It should be borne in mind that this restriction on recovering costs applies only where the opponent actually was legally aided. The fact that he was sufficiently impecunious to be financially eligible for legal aid will not normally affect the operation of the court's discretion on costs. Nor should the assisted person be protected in respect of costs the other party incurred before the assisted person was granted legal aid. If the assisted person has taken steps outside the scope of his certificate, such as counterclaiming when he had legal aid only to defend, then he will not be protected from a costs order in respect of that. In practice, though, these points are rarely taken by successful parties.

7.3.3 Recovering costs against the legal aid fund

Where the provisions of s 11 of the Access to Justice Act 1999 have prevented a successful party recovering his costs from his opponent, it may be possible to recover them from the legal aid fund itself. The relevant provisions are the Community Legal Services (Costs Protection Regulations) Regulations 2000 (SI 2000/824). The conditions that must be satisfied by the party seeking the award are that:

(a) he did not commence the action (this would seem to exclude a person who has successfully defended a counterclaim from benefiting);

(b) he was unassisted (it is somewhat anomalous that a successful assisted person who has paid a contribution and/or is subject to the statutory charge cannot benefit from this provision);

(c) it is just and equitable for the court to make the award; and

(d) he would suffer severe financial hardship if the award were not made. This stipulation has been interpreted quite liberally as applying to potentially benefit all but the very wealthy (*Hanning v Maitland (No 2)* [1970] 1 QB 580, CA).

It may be possible for a landlord to recover his costs from the legal aid fund where he has successfully resisted a claim by a legally aided tenant – for instance, for wrongful eviction. Where an order is sought under the Regulations, the normal procedure is for the application to be made at the end of the trial. The judge will, if so inclined, make a provisional award under the section, giving the Legal Services Commission an opportunity to make representation if it wishes before the order becomes final. However, the application can be made for three months afterwards.

7.4   Court fees

Listed below are the amounts of the fees most likely to be incurred in respect of a county court action of the type that is the subject of this book. When a solicitor is acting for a legally aided person he should look to the Legal Services Commission rather than his client for reimbursement of these. The court does have a discretion to waive fees in the case of people receiving means tested social security benefits or in other instances of exceptional hardship.

Issuing possession proceedings	£120	
Money claims of not more than	£200	£27
	£300	£38
	£400	£50
	£500	£60
	£1,000	£80
	£5,000	£115
	£15,000	£230
	£50,000	£350
an unlimited amount		£500

A further £80 has to be paid on the case's allocation, unless it is only for money and for less than £1,000. A £300 trial fee has to be paid for multi-track cases, and £200 for fast track cases. There is no trial fee for small claims.

8 Suggested Forms and Precedents

8.1 Agreement for a residential tenancy

This agreement is made on [1 November 2000] between: [RB] (hereinafter called the landlord) for one part and [BA and JW] (hereinafter called the tenants) for the other part AND IT IS AGREED as follows:

1. The landlord lets to the tenants the premises known as [9, Eden Park, Auckland, County Durham] together with the fixtures, fittings, furniture and effects therein (hereinafter called the contents) which are specified in the attached inventory signed by the landlord and the tenants for a term of [12 months] (hereinafter called the term) commencing on the [21 November 2000] at a rent of [£250] per [month] to be paid in advance on the [20th] day of each [month] except that the first such payment shall be due on the date hereof.

The tenants agree to:

(i) pay the rent on the days and in the manner as aforesaid;

(ii) pay for all gas and electricity consumed or supplied on or to the premises (including all fixed and standing charges) and to pay all charges for the maintenance and use of the 'land line' telephone on the premises during the term;

(iii) keep the interior of the premises clean and tidy and in as good and tenantable state of repair and decorative condition as at the beginning of the term, reasonable wear and tear and damage by fire excepted;

(iv) not damage or injure the premises;

(v) use the premises in and only in a tenant-like manner;

(vi) keep the contents clean, in good repair and condition and where applicable in working order, reasonable wear and tear and damage by fire being excepted;

(vii) replace any of the contents which may be destroyed or damaged so as to be unusable other than through fair wear and tear or by fire with others of similar value and appearance;

[(viii) keep the garden clean and tidy and in a proper state of cultivation;]

(ix) not remove any of the contents from the premises;

(x) not carry on any trade, business or profession upon the premises nor receive paying guests but use the premises only as a private residence for a maximum of [two] residents;

(xi) not exhibit any poster or notice so as to be visible from the exterior of the premises;

(xii) not permit or allow to be done on the premises anything which may be or become a nuisance or annoyance to the landlord or the occupiers of any adjoining premises or which may render the landlord's insurance of the premises void or voidable or increase the rate of premium for such insurance;

(xiii) not use or allow the premises to be used for any illegal or immoral purpose;

(xiv) not make any noise or play any radio, television set, record player, tape player, musical instrument or similar device at the premises between 11 pm and 8 am so as to be audible outside the premises;

(xv) not block or cause any blockage to the drains and pipe gutters and channels in or about the premises;

(xvi) not assign, underlet or part with possession of the whole or any part of the premises;

(xvii) permit the landlord and the landlord's agents at reasonable times in daylight by appointment to enter the premises during the last 28 days of the term with prospective tenants and during any part of the term with prospective purchasers of the landlord's interest in the premises;

(xviii) notify the landlord forthwith in writing of any defects in the premises as soon as practicable after such defects come to the notice of the tenant; and

(xix) at the end of the term:

> (a) yield up the premises and the contents in such state of repair and condition as shall be in accordance with the tenant's obligations under this agreement;

> (b) make good or pay for the repair or replacement of such of the contents as have been broken, lost or damaged during the term other than through fair wear and tear or by fire;

> (c) pay for the washing (including ironing and pressing) of all linen and for the washing and cleaning (including ironing and pressing) of all blankets and curtains and similar items which have been soiled during the tenancy; and

> (d) leave the contents in the rooms and places in which they were at the commencement of the term.

The landlord agrees to:

(i) pay and indemnify the tenants against all council tax assessments and outgoings and all water and sewerage charges in respect of the premises;

(ii) permit the tenants, so long as they pay the rent and perform their obligations under this agreement, quietly to use and enjoy the premises during the term without any interruption from the landlord or any person rightfully claiming under or in trust for the landlord;

(iii) return to the tenants any rent payable for any period during which the premises may have been rendered uninhabitable by fire or any other risk against which the landlord has insured.

If:

(i) any part of the rent is in arrears for more than 14 days whether formally demanded or not; or

(ii) if there is any breach of any of the tenants' obligations under this agreement; or

(iii) if the premises are without the agreement of the landlord left unoccupied for a continuous period in excess of four weeks,

the landlord may re-enter the premises and thereupon the tenancy created by this agreement will determine, but without prejudice to any other rights and remedies of the landlord.

The landlord acknowledges the receipt from the tenants of the sum of £250 by way of deposit and agrees to repay the same to the tenants along with such interest as will have accrued from placing the said deposit in a seven day deposit account with [Whichever] Bank at the end of the term after deducting all arrears of rent and other sums which may then be due from the tenants to the landlord as a result of any breach by the tenant of any of the tenants' obligations under this agreement. The tenants are not entitled to repayment of the deposit or any part thereof until possession shall be yielded up to the landlord.

Signed by the landlord

Landlord's signature witnessed by [name and address]

[Signature of witness]

Signed by tenants

Tenants' signature witnessed by [name and address]

[Signature of witness]

Note: This example is for use where the tenancy is for a fixed term, with rent payable monthly, and is furnished. It can be adapted quite simply where the terms are different. It will normally have the effect of creating an assured shorthold tenancy.

8.2   Agreement for a residential tenancy which is not an assured shorthold tenancy due to the landlord residing in the same building

This agreement is made on [9 October 2000] between: [BL] (hereinafter called 'the lessor') for one part, and [RH] (hereinafter called 'the lessee') for the other part.

IT IS AGREED as follows:

That the lessor will allow the lessee to occupy the basement flat in the premises known as and situate at [100 Grace Road, Leicester] (the said flat hereinafter being referred to as 'the premises') and have the use of the fixtures, fittings, furniture and effects therein which are specified in the attached inventory signed by the lessor and the lessee and collectively referred to herein as 'the contents' for a term of [six months] (hereinafter called the term) commencing on [12 October 2000] in consideration for the payment by the lessee of a fee of [£250] per month to be paid in advance on the 11th day of each month save that the first such payment is to be made on the date hereof.

The lessee agrees to:

(i) pay the fee on the days and in the manner aforesaid;

(ii) pay for all gas and electricity consumed or supplied on or to the premises (including all fixed and standing charges) and all charges for the maintenance and use of the telephone on the premises during the term;

(iii) keep the interior of the premises clean and tidy and in as good a state of repair and decorative order as at the beginning of the term, fair wear and tear and damage by fire excepted;

(iv) not damage or injure the premises;

(v) use the premises only in a responsible manner, having regard to the proximity of the lessor in the other parts of the said 100 Grace Road, and in particular will not:

   (a) at any time play a radio, record or tape player, television, musical instrument or similar apparatus so that it can be heard in the other parts of the said 100 Grace Road or so that it causes nuisance or annoyance to anyone not on the premises;

   (b) at any time have more than eight people, including the lessee, in the premises; and

   (c) between the hours of midnight and 8 am have more than two people, including the lessee, in the premises;

(vi) keep the contents clean, in good repair and where applicable working order; reasonable wear and tear, mechanical breakdown not caused by misuse, and fire damage being excepted;

(vii) replace any of the contents which may be destroyed or damaged in breach of clause (vii) above;

(viii) not remove any of the contents from the premises or from the respective positions in the premises which they occupy at the commencement of the term;

(ix) not carry on any trade, business or profession upon the premises nor receive paying guests but use the premises only as a private residence for the lessee only;

(x) not exhibit any poster or notice so as to be visible from the exterior of the premises;

(xi) not use the premises for any illegal or immoral purpose;

(xii) permit the lessor to enter the premises at any hour for any purpose;

(xiii) at the end of the term yield up the premises and contents in such state of repair and condition as shall be in accordance with the lessees' obligations under this agreement.

The lessor agrees to:

(i) pay and indemnify the lessee against all council tax assessments and outgoings and all water and sewerage charges in respect of the premises;

(ii) change the bed linen on the bed in the premises at least once during every week of the term.

This agreement is personal to the lessee and may not be assigned by [him] and will terminate automatically if the lessee ceases to reside at the premises.

If any part of the fee is not paid and becomes more than 14 days in arrears (whether or not formally demanded) or if the lessee breaches any of [his] obligations under this agreement the tenant will be deemed to have forfeited his right to occupy the premises and the lessor may treat the premises as no longer occupied by the lessee whereupon all rights the lessee has under this agreement will terminate, without prejudice to any of the lessor's other rights under this agreement.

The lessee will on the date hereof pay to the lessor a deposit of [£250] which the lessor hereby acknowledges. This deposit will be repaid to the lessee when and only when he quits the premises. It will then be repaid without interest and less any outstanding amounts of fee owed under this agreement or in respect of occupation by the tenant after the expiry of this agreement and any other sums that may be due from the lessee to the lessor under the terms of this agreement.

Signed by the lessor

Lessor's signature witnessed by [name and address]

[Signature of witness]

Signed by lessee

Lessee's signature witnessed by [name and address]

[Signature of witness]

Note: This example is in many ways not dissimilar to that used for an assured shorthold tenancy. The main differences arise out of the need to use language which commits the lessor to a tenancy, rather than a licence, and the fact that the parties to the agreement will live in much closer proximity than where there is a tenancy with an absentee landlord.

8.3 Endorsement on a tenancy agreement which is to be subject to Grounds 1 and 2 of Sched 2 to the HA 1988, where landlord has previously lived in the property

To the tenant [PJ]: TAKE NOTICE that the landlord, [PC], has at some time before the beginning of this tenancy occupied the dwelling house which is the subject of this tenancy as his only or principal residence and may recover possession thereof under the provisions of Ground 1 of Sched 2 to the Housing Act 1988. AND FURTHER TAKE NOTICE that the dwelling house which is the subject of the tenancy is subject to a mortgage granted to the [Whichever] Building Society/Bank and that under the said mortgage the said Building Society/Bank may in certain circumstances be entitled to exercise a power of sale conferred on it by the mortgage and/or section 101 of the Law of Property Act 1925 and the said Building Society may recover possession thereof in pursuance of that power under the provisions of Ground 2 of the Housing Act 1988.

Signed [Landlord or agent]

I/we acknowledge receipt of a notice of which this is a true copy

Signed [tenant]

8.4 Endorsement on a tenancy agreement which is to be subject to Grounds 1 and 2 of Sched 2 to the HA 1988, where landlord has not previously lived in the property

To the tenant [RB]: TAKE NOTICE that the landlord [KS] may in due course require the dwelling as his or his spouse's only or principal home and that in such event may recover possession thereof under the provisions of Ground 3 of Schedule 2 to the Housing Act 1988.

AND FURTHER TAKE NOTICE [continue as in 8.3 above] ...

8.5 Notice that tenancy is not to be an assured shorthold tenancy, served on tenant before tenancy commences

Take notice:

To: Graham Swan,

The tenancy of 101 Wantage Road, Northampton which is to be granted to you commencing on 1 December 2000 is not to be an assured shorthold tenancy.

Signed [landlord]

8.6 Notice of landlord's address

Section 48 of the Landlord and Tenant Act 1987

To the tenant: [name and address of premises]

Please note that the address at which notices concerning the above property, including notices in proceedings, may be served on your landlord [landlord's name] is [landlord's address]

Signed [landlord or agent]

8.7 Notice to quit addressed to a tenant

NOTICE TO QUIT (SERVED BY LANDLORD'S AGENT)

To [Co] of [68 Sabina Park, Kingston, Surrey]:

We [name of agent giving notice] on behalf of your landlord(s) [JH] of 1, The Hill, Sydenham, London], give you notice to quit and deliver up possession to him of [68 Sabina Park, Kingston, Surrey] on 24 January 2001 or the day on which a complete period of your tenancy expires next after the end of four weeks from the service of this notice.

Date [18 December 2000]

Signed [Solicitor or other agent]

The name and address of the agent who served this notice is [Bairstow and Blakey, 46 Trent Bridge, Nottingham].

Information for tenant

1. If the tenant or licensee does not leave the dwelling, the landlord or licensor must get an order for possession from the court before the tenant or licensee can lawfully be evicted. The landlord or licensor cannot apply for such an order before the notice to quit or notice to determine has run out.

2. A tenant or licensee who does not know if he has any right to remain in possession after a notice to determine runs out can obtain advice from a solicitor. Help with all or part of the cost of legal advice and assistance may be available under the Legal Aid Scheme. He should also be able to obtain information from a Citizens' Advice Bureau, a Housing Aid Centre or a rent officer.

Notes:

1 Notice to quit any premises let as a dwelling must be given at least four weeks before it takes effect and it must be in writing (s 5 of the Protection from Eviction Act 1977).

2 Where a notice to quit is given by a landlord to determine a tenancy of any premises let as a dwelling, the notice must contain this information (Notice to Quit etc (Prescribed Information) Regulations 1988 (SI 1988/2201)).

8.8   Landlord's notice proposing a new rent under an assured periodic tenancy or agricultural occupancy

Statutory Instrument 1997 No. 194
The Assured Tenancies and Agricultural Occupancies (Forms) Regulations 1997 - *continued*

FORM No. 4

Housing Act 1988 section 13(2)

Landlord's Notice proposing a new rent under an Assured Periodic Tenancy or Agricultural Occupancy

- Please write clearly in black ink.

- Please tick boxes where appropriate.

- This form should be used to propose a new rent under an assured periodic tenancy, including an assured shorthold periodic tenancy.

- This form may also be used to propose a new rent or licence fee for an assured periodic agricultural occupancy. In such cases reference to "landlord"/"tenant" can be read as references to "licensor"/"licensee" etc

- Do not use this form if there is a current rent fixing mechanism in the tenancy.

- Do not use this form to propose a rent adjustment for a statutory periodic tenancy solely because of a proposed change of terms under section 6(2) of the Housing Act 1988. You should instead use the form headed *Notice proposing different terms for a Statutory Periodic Tenancy* which you can obtain from a rent assessment panel or a law stationer.

1. To:

Name(s) of tenant(s)

2. Address of premises to which the tenancy relates:

3. This is to give notice that as from .... your landlord proposes to charge a new rent.

• The new rent must take effect at the beginning of a new period of the tenancy and not earlier than any of the following:

(a) the minimum period after this notice was served,

(The minimum period is:

- in the case of a yearly tenancy, six months;

- in the case of a tenancy where the period is less than a month, one month;

- in any other case, a period equal to the period of the tenancy;)

(b) the first anniversary of the start of the first period of the tenancy except in the case of:

- a statutory periodic tenancy, which arises when a fixed term assured tenancy ends, or;

- an assured tenancy which arose on the death of a tenant under a regulated tenancy;

(c) if the rent under the tenancy has previously been increased by a notice under section 13 or a determination under section 14 of the Housing Act 1988, the first anniversary of the date on which the increased rent took effect.

4.

(a) The existing rent is: £ _____   per _____

(e.g. week, month, year)

(b) Does the rent include council tax?   Yes ☐   No ☐

(c) If yes, the amount that is included for council tax is: £ _____   per _____

(e.g. week, month, year)

(d) Does the rent include water charges?   Yes ☐   No ☐

(e) If yes, the amount that is included for water charges is: £ _____   per _____

(e.g. week, month, year)

5.

(a) The proposed new rent will be: £ _____   per _____

(e.g. week, month, year)

(b) Will the new rent include council tax?   Yes ❏   No ❏

(c) If yes, the amount that will be included for council tax will be: £ _____   per _____

(e.g. week, month, year)

(d) Will the new rent include water charges?   Yes ❏   No ❏

(e) If yes, the amount that will be included for water charges will be: £ _____   per _____

(e.g. week, month, year)

6. Name and address of landlord.

To be signed and dated by the landlord or his agent (someone acting for him). If there are joint landlords each landlord or the agent must sign unless one signs on behalf of the rest with their agreement.

Signed _____   *Date* _____

_____

Please specify whether: landlord ❏ joint landlords ❏ landlord's agent ❏

Name(s) (Block Capitals)

_____

_____

Address

_____

_____

Telephone - Daytime _____   Evening _____

What to do if this notice is served on you

- You should read this notice carefully. Your landlord is proposing a new rent.

- If you agree with the new rent proposed, do nothing. If you do not agree and you are unable to reach agreement with your landlord or do not want to discuss it directly with him, you may refer this notice to your local rent assessment committee prior to the date specified in section 3, using the form headed *Application referring a Notice proposing a new rent under an Assured Periodic Tenancy or Agricultural Occupancy to a Rent Assessment Committee.* You can obtain this form from a rent assessment panel or a law stationer.

- The rent assessment committee will consider your application and will decide what the rent for the premises will be. The committee may set a rent that is higher, lower or the same as the landlord has proposed in section 5.

- If you are required to include payments for council tax and water charges in your rent, the rent the committee determines will be inclusive of council tax and water charges.

- If you need help or advice please take this notice immediately to a citizens advice bureau, a housing advice centre, a law centre or a solicitor.

8.9   Notice of reference of a proposed rent increase to a rent assessment committee

Statutory Instrument 1997 No. 194
The Assured Tenancies and Agricultural Occupancies (Forms) Regulations 1997 - *continued*

FORM No. 5

Housing Act 1988 section 13(4)

Application referring a Notice proposing a new rent under an Assured Periodic Tenancy or Agricultural Occupancy to a Rent Assessment Committee

- Please write clearly in black ink

- Please tick boxes where appropriate and cross out text marked with an asterisk (*) that does not apply.

- This form should be used when your landlord has served notice on you proposing a new rent under an assured periodic tenancy, including an assured shorthold periodic tenancy

- This form may also be used to refer a notice proposing a new rent or licence fee for an assured periodic agricultural occupancy. In such a case references to "landlord"/"tenant" can be read as references to "licensor"/ "licensee" etc.

- This form must be completed and sent to your local rent assessment panel - with a copy of the notice served on you proposing the new rent - before the date it is proposed that the new rent will take effect.

1. Address of premises:

_____

_____

_____

_____

2. Name(s) of landlord(s)/agent* :

_____

Address of landlord(s)/agent* :

_____

_____

_____

_____

3. Details of premises.

(a) What type of accommodation do you rent?

Room(s) ❏   Flat ❏   Terraced House ❏

Semi-Detached House ❏   Fully Detached House ❏   Other *(Please specify)* ❏

(b) If it is a flat or room(s) what floor(s) is it on?

Ground ❏ First ❏ Second ❏ Other ❏ *(Please specify)*

(c) Give the number and type of rooms, eg living room, bathroom etc.

_____
_____

(d) Does the tenancy include any other facilities, eg garden, garage or other separate building or land?

Yes ❏ No ❏

(e) If yes, please give details:

_____
_____

(f) Do you share any accommodation with

(i) the landlord?   Yes ❏   No ❏

(ii) another tenant or tenants?   Yes ❏   No ❏

(g) If yes to either of the above, please give details:

_____
_____

4. When did the present tenancy begin?

5.

(a) Did you pay a premium?

Yes ❏ No ❏

• a premium is a payment which is additional to rent and is equivalent to more than two months rent. It may give you the right to assign the tenancy (pass it on to someone else) unless the tenancy agreement states or implies otherwise.

(b) If yes, please give details:

_____
_____
_____

6. Services

(a) Are any services provided under the tenancy (eg cleaning, lighting, heating, hot water or gardening)?

Yes ☐ No ☐

(b) If yes, please give details:

_____
_____
_____

(c) If yes, is a separate charge made for services, maintenance, repairs, landlord's costs of management or any other item?

Yes ☐ No ☐

(d) What charge is payable?

£............. per ....
(e.g. week, month, year)

(e) Does the charge vary according to the relevant costs?

Yes ☐ No ☐

(f) If yes, please give details:

_____
_____
_____

7.

(a) Is any furniture provided under the tenancy?

Yes ☐ No ☐

(b) If yes, please give details. Continue on a separate sheet if necessary or attach a copy of the inventory:

_____
_____
_____

8. Improvements

(a) Have you, or any former tenant(s) carried out improvements or replaced fixtures, fittings or furniture for which you or they were not responsible under the terms of the tenancy?

Yes ☐ No ☐

(b) If yes, please give details. Continue on a separate sheet if necessary:

_____
_____
_____

9. What repairs are the responsibility of:

    (a) the landlord?

_____

_____

_____

    (b) the tenant?

_____

_____

_____

10.

    (a) Is there a written tenancy agreement?   Yes ☐   No ☐

    (b) If yes, please attach the tenancy agreement (with a note of any variations). It will be returned to you as soon as possible.

11. Do you have an assured agricultural occupancy?

    Yes ☐   No ☐

12.

    (a) I/we* attach a copy of the notice proposing a new rent under the assured periodic tenancy and I/we* apply for it to be considered by the rent assessment committee.

    Signed   *Date*

_____   _____

_____

_____

To be signed and dated by the tenant or his agent. If there are joint tenants each tenant or the agent must sign unless one signs on behalf of the rest with their agreement.

Please specify whether: tenant ☐   joint tenants ☐   tenant's agent ☐

    (b) Name and address of tenant(s) referring to the rent assessment committee.

Name(s) (Block Capitals)

_____

_____

_____

Address

_____

_____

Telephone - Daytime

_____

8.10 Application to a Rent Assessment Committee for a determination of a rent under an assured shorthold tenancy

Statutory Instrument 1997 No. 194
The Assured Tenancies and Agricultural Occupancies (Forms) Regulations 1997 - *continued*

FORM No. 6

Housing Act 1988 section 22(1) as amended by section 100 of the Housing Act 1996

Application to a Rent Assessment Committee for a determination of a rent under an Assured Shorthold Tenancy

- Please write clearly in black ink.

- Please tick boxes where appropriate and cross out text marked with an asterisk (*) that does not apply.

- This form should be used by a tenant with an assured shorthold tenancy which began (or for which a contract had been made) before 28th February 1997, to apply to the local rent assessment committee, during the fixed term of the original tenancy, to have the rent reduced.

- This form should also be used by a tenant with an assured shorthold tenancy which began on or after 28th February 1997 (unless a contract had been made before that date), to apply to the rent assessment committee within six months of the beginning of the original tenancy, to have the rent reduced.

- This form cannot be used in the cases specified at the end of this form.

- When you have completed the form please send it to your local rent assessment panel.

1. Address of premises:

2. Name(s) of landlord(s)/agent*

Address of landlord(s)/agent*

3. Details of premises.

    (a) What type of accommodation do you rent?

        Room(s) ❐   Flat ❐   Terraced House ❐

        Semi-Detached House ❐   Fully Detached House ❐   Other ❐ *(Please specify)*

    (b) If it is a flat or room(s) what floor(s) is it on?

        Ground ❐ First ❐ Second ❐ Other ❐ *(Please specify)*

    (c) Give the number and type of rooms, eg living room, bathroom etc.

    _____

    (d) Does the tenancy include any other facilities, eg garden, garage or other separate building or land?

        Yes ❐ No ❐

    (e) If yes, please give details:

    _____
    _____
    _____

    (f) Do you share any accommodation with:

        (i) the landlord?   Yes ❐   No ❐

        (ii) another tenant or tenants?   Yes ❐   No ❐

    (g) If yes to either of the above, please give details:

_____
_____
_____

4.
(a) What is the current rent?   £ _____   per _____

                                                             (e.g. week, month, year)

(b) Does the rent include council tax?   Yes ☐   No ☐

(c) If yes, the amount that is included for council tax is: £ _____   per _____

                                                             (e.g. week, month, year)

(d) Does the rent include water charges?   Yes ☐   No ☐

(e) If yes, the amount that is included for water charges is: £ _____   per _____

                                                             (e.g. week, month, year)

5.
(a) When did the present tenancy begin?

_____

(b) When does the present tenancy end?

_____

(c) Does the tenancy replace an original tenancy?   Yes ☐   No ☐

If yes, when did the original tenancy begin

_____

6.
(a) If the tenancy began before 28th February 1997, please confirm by ticking the box that you received a notice saying that the tenancy was to be an assured shorthold tenancy before the agreement was entered into. ☐

(b) Attach a copy of the notice, if available. It will be returned to you as soon as possible.

7.
(a) Did you pay a premium?

Yes ☐ No ☐

• a premium is a payment which is additional to rent and is equivalent to more than two months rent. It may give you the right to assign the tenancy (pass it on to someone else) unless the tenancy agreement states or implies otherwise.

(b) If yes, please give details:

_____
_____
_____

8. Services.

(a) Are any services provided under the tenancy (eg cleaning, lighting, heating, hot water or gardening)?

Yes ❏ No ❏

(b) If yes, please give details:

_____

_____

_____

(c) Is a separate charge made for services, maintenance, repairs, landlord's costs of management or any other item?

Yes ❏ No ❏

(d) If yes, what charge is payable?   £ _____   per _____

(e.g. week, month, year)

(e) Does the charge vary according to the relevant costs?

Yes ❏ No ❏

(f) If yes, please give details:

_____

_____

_____

9.

(a) Is any furniture provided under the tenancy?

Yes ❏ No ❏

(b) If yes, please give details. Continue on a separate sheet if necessary or provide a copy of the inventory.

_____

_____

_____

10. What repairs are the responsibility of:

(a) the landlord. Continue on a separate sheet if necessary:

_____

_____

_____

(b) the tenant. Continue on a separate sheet if necessary:

_____

_____

_____

11.

(a) Give details (if known) of the other terms of the tenancy, eg whether the tenancy is assignable and whether a premium may be charged on an assignment. (Continue on a separate sheet if necessary).

....

....

....

(b) Is there a written tenancy agreement?   Yes ☐   No ☐

(c) If yes, please attach the tenancy agreement (with a note of any variations). It will be returned to you as soon as possible.

12.

(a) I/We* apply to the rent assessment committee to determine a rent for the above mentioned premises.

Signed   *Date*

....

....

To be signed and dated by the tenant or his agent. If there are joint tenants each tenant or the agent must sign unless one signs on behalf of the rest with their agreement.

Please specify whether: tenant ☐ joint tenants ☐ tenant's agent ☐

(b) Name and address of tenant(s) referring to the rent assessment committee.

Name(s) (Block Capitals)

....

....

Address

....

....

Telephone ;- Daytime

....

Cases where this form should not be used
• An application cannot be made if -

(a) the rent payable under the tenancy is a rent previously determined by a rent assessment committee; or

(b) the tenancy is a replacement tenancy and more than six months have elapsed since the beginning of the original tenancy. A replacement tenancy is an assured shorthold tenancy that came into being on the ending of a tenancy which had been an assured shorthold of the same, or substantially the same, property and the landlord and tenant under each tenancy were the same at that time.

• The rent assessment committee cannot make a determination unless it considers -

(a) that there is a sufficient number of similar properties in the locality let on assured tenancies (whether shorthold or not) for comparison; and

(b) that the rent payable under the shorthold tenancy in question is significantly higher than the rent which the landlord might reasonably be expected to get in comparison with other rents for similar properties let on assured tenancies (whether shorthold or not) in the locality.

8.11 Notice proposing different terms for statutory periodic tenancy

Statutory Instrument 1997 No. 194
The Assured Tenancies and Agricultural Occupancies (Forms)
Regulations 1997 - *continued*

SCHEDULE   egulatioıR3

FORMS PRESCRIBED FOR THE PURPOSES OF PART I OF THE
HOUSING ACT 1988

FORM No. 1

Housing Act 1988 section 6(2)

Notice proposing different terms for a Statutory Periodic Tenancy

- Please write clearly in black ink.

- Please tick boxes where appropriate and cross out text marked with an asterisk (*) that does not apply.

- This form can be used by either a landlord or a tenant to propose changes to the terms of a statutory periodic tenancy, which arises when a fixed term of an assured tenancy, an assured shorthold tenancy or an assured agricultural occupancy ends.

- This notice must be served on the landlord or tenant no later than the first anniversary of the day on which the former fixed term tenancy or occupancy ended.

- Do not use this notice if you are a landlord proposing only an increase in rent. Instead, you should use the form headed *Landlord's Notice proposing a new rent under an Assured Periodic Tenancy or Agricultural Occupancy*, which is *available from a rent assessment panel or law stationers.*

1. To:
....

*Name(s) of landlord(s)/tenant(s)**

Address of premises to which the tenancy relates:
....
....
....

2. This is to give notice that I/we* propose different terms for the statutory periodic tenancy from those of the fixed term assured tenancy which has now ended and that they should take effect from:

....

Insert date which must be at least three months after the date on which this notice is served.

3. Changes to the terms

(a) The existing provisions of the tenancy to be changed are:

....
....

(b) The proposed changes are:

_____

_____

_____

Continue on a separate sheet if necessary

4. Changes to the rent (if applicable). Go to section 5 if this does not apply.

• You should not propose a change to the rent on this form unless it is to take account of the proposed new terms at section 3. A change may be made if either the landlord or the tenant considers it appropriate.

(a) The existing rent is   £ _____   per _____

                                                                  (e.g. week, month, year)

(b) Does the rent include council tax?   Yes ❑   No ❑

(c) If yes, the amount that is included for council tax is: £ _____   per _____

                                                                  (e.g. week, month, year)

(d) Does the rent include water charges?   Yes ❑   No ❑

(e) If yes, the amount that is included for water charges is: £ _____   per _____

                                                                  (e.g. week, month, year)

(f) The new rent which takes into account the proposed changes in the terms of the tenancy will be: £ _____   per _____

                                                                  (e.g. week, month, year)

(g) Will the new rent include council tax?   Yes ❑   No ❑

(h) If yes, the amount that will be included for council tax is: £ _____   per _____

                                                                  (e.g. week, month, year)

(i) Will the new rent include water charges?   Yes ❑   No ❑

(j) If yes, the amount that will be included for water charges is: £ _____   per _____

5. Name and address of landlord or tenant proposing the changes

To be signed and dated by the landlord or his agent (someone acting for him) or the tenant or his agent. If there are joint landlords or joint tenants each landlord/tenant or the agent must sign unless one signs on behalf of the rest with their agreement.

Signed

Date

Please specify whether: landlord ❐ landlord's agent ❐ tenant ❐ tenant's agent ❐

Name(s) (Block Capitals)

Address

Telephone - Daytime

Evening

What to do if this notice is served on you

- If you agree with the new terms and rent proposed, do nothing. They will become the terms of the tenancy agreement on the date specified in section 2.

- If you don't agree with the proposed terms and any adjustment of the rent (see section 4), and you are unable to reach agreement with your landlord/tenant, or you do not wish to discuss it with him, you may refer the matter directly to your local rent assessment committee, before the date specified in section 2, using the form headed *Application referring a Notice proposing different terms for a Statutory Periodic Tenancy to a Rent Assessment Committee* which you can obtain from a rent assessment panel or a law stationer.

- The rent assessment committee will decide what, if any, changes should be made to the terms of the tenancy and, if applicable, the amount of the new rent.

- If you need help or advice about this notice and what you should do about it, take it immediately to a citizens advice bureau, a housing advice centre, a law centre or a solicitor.

8.12 Application referring a notice proposing different terms for a statutory periodic tenancy to a rent assessment committee

Statutory Instrument 1997 No. 194
The Assured Tenancies and Agricultural Occupancies (Forms) Regulations 1997 - continued

FORM No. 2

Housing Act 1988 section 6(3)

Application referring a Notice proposing different terms for a Statutory Periodic Tenancy to a Rent Assessment Committee

- Please write clearly in black ink.

- Please tick boxes where appropriate and cross out text marked with an asterisk (*) that does not apply.

- This form should be used by a landlord or a tenant who has been served with a notice under section 6(2) of the Housing Act 1988, varying the terms of a statutory

periodic tenancy which arises when a fixed term of an assured tenancy, an assured shorthold tenancy or an assured agricultural occupancy ends.

- When you have completed the form, please send it to your local rent assessment panel with a copy of the notice served on you proposing the new terms of the statutory periodic tenancy.

1. Name(s) of tenant(s):

2. Address of premises to which the tenancy relates:

3. Name(s) of landlord(s)/agent*:

Address of landlord(s)/agent*:

4. Details of premises.

(a) What type of accommodation is rented?

Room(s) ❏   Flat ❏   Terraced House ❏

Semi-Detached House ❏   Fully Detached House ❏   Other ❏(Please specify)

(b) If it is a flat or room(s) what floor(s) is it on?

Ground ❏ First ❏ Second ❏ Other ❏ (Please specify)

(c) Give the number and type of rooms, eg living room, bathroom etc.

_____

_____

(d) Does the tenancy include any other facilities, eg garden, garage or other separate building or land?

Yes ❏ No ❏

(e) If yes, please give details:

_____

_____

_____

(f) Is any of the accommodation shared with:

(i) the landlord?   Yes ❏   No ❏

(ii) another tenant or tenants?   Yes ❏   No ❏

(g) If yes, please give details:

_____

_____

_____

5. When did the statutory periodic tenancy begin?

_____

6. Services.

(a) Are any services provided under the tenancy (eg cleaning, lighting, heating, hot water or gardening etc.)?

Yes ☐ No ☐

(b) If yes, please give details:

_____

_____

_____

(c) Is a separate charge made for services, maintenance, repairs, landlords' costs of management or any other item?

Yes ☐ No ☐

(d) If yes, what charge is payable?　　　　　　　£ _____　per _____

(e.g. week, month, year)

(e) Does the charge vary according to the relevant costs?　　Yes ☐　　No ☐

(f) If yes, please give details:

_____

_____

_____

7.

(a) Is any furniture provided under the tenancy?

Yes ☐ No ☐

(b) If yes, please give details. Continue on a separate sheet if necessary or provide a copy of the inventory.

_____

_____

_____

8. What repairs are the responsibility of:

(a) the landlord? Continue on a separate sheet if necessary.

_____

_____

_____

(b) the tenant? Continue on a separate sheet if necessary.

_____

_____

_____

9. Give details (if known) of the other terms of the tenancy, e.g. can you assign the tenancy (pass it on to someone else) and if so is a premium (a payment which is in addition to rent and equivalent to more than two months rent) payable on an assignment? Continue on a separate sheet if necessary.

10.

(a) Is there a written tenancy agreement? Yes ☐ No ☐

(b) If yes, please attach the tenancy agreement (with a note of any variations). It will be returned to you as soon as possible.

11.

(a) I/We* attach a copy of the notice proposing changes to the statutory periodic tenancy and, if applicable, an adjustment of the amount of rent and apply for it to be considered by the rent assessment committee.

Signed

Date

To be signed and dated by the landlord or his agent (someone acting for him) or the tenant or his agent. If there are joint landlords or joint tenants each landlord/tenant or the agent must sign unless one signs on behalf of the rest with their agreement.

Please specify whether: landlord ☐ landlord's agent ☐ tenant ☐ tenant's agent ☐

(b) Name and address of landlord or tenant referring to the rent assessment committee.

Name(s) (Block Capitals)

Address

Telephone - Daytime

8.13 Notice to an assured tenant that the landlord requires possession

Statutory Instrument 1997 No. 194
The Assured Tenancies and Agricultural Occupancies (Forms)
Regulations 1997 - *continued*

FORM No. 3

Housing Act 1988 section 8 as amended by section 151 of the Housing Act 1996

Notice seeking possession of a property let on an Assured Tenancy or an Assured Agricultural Occupancy

- Please write clearly in black ink.

- Please tick boxes where appropriate and cross out text marked with an asterisk (*) that does not apply.

- This form should be used where possession of accommodation let under an assured tenancy, an assured agricultural occupancy or an assured shorthold tenancy is sought on one of the grounds in Schedule 2 to the Housing Act 1988.

- Do not use this form if possession is sought on the "shorthold" ground under section 21 of the Housing Act 1988 from an assured shorthold tenant where the fixed term has come to an end or, for assured shorthold tenancies with no fixed term which started on or after 28th February 1997, after six months has elapsed. There is no prescribed form for these cases, but you must give notice in writing.

1. To:

Name(s) of tenant(s)/licensee(s)*

2. Your landlord/licensor* intends to apply to the court for an order requiring you to give up possession of:

Address of premises

3. Your landlord/licensor* intends to seek possession on ground(s) .... in Schedule 2 to the Housing Act 1988, as amended by the Housing Act 1996, which read(s):

Give the full text (as set out in the Housing Act 1988 as amended by the Housing Act 1996) of each ground which is being relied on. Continue on a separate sheet if necessary.

4. Give a full explanation of why each ground is being relied on:

....

....

....

Continue on a separate sheet if necessary.

Notes on the grounds for possession

- If the court is satisfied that any of grounds 1 to 8 is established, it must make an order (but see below in respect of fixed term tenancies).

- Before the court will grant an order on any of grounds 9 to 17, it must be satisfied that it is reasonable to require you to leave. This means that, if one of these grounds is set out in section 3, you will be able to suggest to the court that it is not reasonable that you should have to leave, even if you accept that the ground applies.

- The court will not make an order under grounds 1, 3 to 7, 9 or 16, to take effect during the fixed term of the tenancy (if there is one) and it will only make an order during the fixed term on grounds 2, 8, 10 to 15 or 17 if the terms of the tenancy make provision for it to be brought to an end on any of these grounds.

- Where the court makes an order for possession solely on ground 6 or 9, the landlord must pay your reasonable removal expenses.

5. The court proceedings will not begin until after:

....

Give the earliest date on which court proceedings can be brought

- Where the landlord is seeking possession on grounds 1, 2, 5 to 7, 9 or 16, court proceedings cannot begin earlier than 2 months from the date this notice is served on you (even where one of grounds 3, 4, 8, 10 to 13, 14A, 15 or 17 is specified) and not before the date on which the tenancy (had it not been assured) could have been brought to an end by a notice to quit served at the same time as this notice.

- Where the landlord is seeking possession on grounds 3, 4, 8, 10 to 13, 14A, 15 or 17, court proceedings cannot begin earlier than 2 weeks from the date this notice is served (unless one of 1, 2, 5 to 7, 9 or 16 grounds is also specified in which case they cannot begin earlier than two months from the date this notice is served).

- Where the landlord is seeking possession on ground 14 (with or without other grounds), court proceedings cannot begin before the date this notice is served.

- Where the landlord is seeking possession on ground 14A, court proceedings cannot begin unless the landlord has served, or has taken all reasonable steps to serve, a copy of this notice on the partner who has left the property.

- After the date shown in section 5, court proceedings may be begun at once but not later than 12 months from the date on which this notice is served. After this time the notice will lapse and a new notice must be served before possession can be sought.

6. Name and address of landlord/licensor* .

To be signed and dated by the landlord or licensor or his agent (someone acting for him). If there are joint landlords each landlord or the agent must sign unless one signs on behalf of the rest with their agreement.

Signed _____   *Date* _____

_____

Please specify whether: landlord ☐ licensor ☐ joint landlords ☐ landlord's agent ☐

Name(s) (Block Capitals)

_____

_____

Address

_____

_____

_____

Telephone - Daytime _____   Evening _____

What to do if this notice is served on you

- This notice is the first step requiring you to give up possession of your home. You should read it very carefully.

- Your landlord cannot make you leave your home without an order for possession issued by a court. By issuing this notice your landlord is informing you that he intends to seek such an order. If you are willing to give up possession without a court order, you should tell the person who signed this notice as soon as possible and say when you are prepared to leave.

- Whichever grounds are set out in section 3 of this form, the court may allow any of the other grounds to be added at a later date. If this is done, you will be told about it so you can discuss the additional grounds at the court hearing as well as the grounds set out in section 3.

- If you need advice about this notice, and what you should do about it, take it immediately to a citizens' advice bureau, a housing advice centre, a law centre or a solicitor.

8.14 Notice terminating an assured shorthold tenancy

To: DB, the tenant of 37 Nevil Road, Bristol,

I, JB, of 92 Trent Bridge, Nottingham, landlord of 37 Nevil Road, Bristol, hereby give you notice that I require possession by virtue of the Housing Act 1988, s 21, of the said 37 Nevil Road on or before 5 March 2001 and that if you do not give up possession of that property to me on or before that date, I shall commence possession proceedings.

Dated 3 January 2001

8.15 Form of particulars of claim in possession actions where arrears of rent are relied upon

See County Court Form N 119 (opposite).

8.16 Application for possession under CCR Ord 24

County Court Form N 312

In the County Court

Case No

In the Matter of [*address of premises*]

Between   AB   Applicant

and

                 CD   Respondent (if any whose name is known to the Applicant)

[*Applicant's name*] of [*address and occupation*] hereby applies to the court for an order for recovery of possession of [*address of property*] on the ground that he is entitled to possession and that the persons[s] in occupation of the premises is [are] in occupation without his licence or consent.

The person[s] in occupation who is [are] intended to be served individually with this application is [are]: [*here state the name of every person in occupation whose name the applicant knows*].

[Add where appropriate: There are other persons in occupation whose names are not known to the applicant.]

[Or: It is not intended to serve any person individually with notice of this application.]

The applicant's address for service is:

[*address for service*].

Dated

I believe/the Claimant believes the facts stated in this application are true

Signed   [solicitors for the] Applicant

8.17 Witness statement in support of originating application under CCR Ord 24

In the   **County Court**

Case No

In the Matter of [*address of premises*]

Between   AB   Applicant

and

                   CD   Respondent (if any whose name
                                    is known to the Applicant)

Statement of [*Applicant*]

1. I make this statement in support of my application for possession of the premises at [*state address*] (hereinafter called 'the premises').

2. I am the freehold owner of the premises having purchased them on 19 March 2000 from the previous owners Mr and Mrs Artemus Jones.

3. I have not yet occupied the premises. They have been vacant since I purchased them, but it is my intention to reside there when I sell my existing home.

4. On 2 June 2000 I visited the property to see that all was well. I found four people inside. I asked who they were and what they were doing there. They refused to give me their names and told me that as I was 'a

filthy capitalist pig' who could 'afford two homes', they had every right to live there and exclude me. I was also told that if I did not leave forthwith I would be physically ejected.

5. I do not know the names of those or of any persons now occupying the premises.

I believe/the Claimant believes the facts stated in this statement are true

Note: In this situation the respondents would have to be described as 'Persons Unknown' on the originating summons. The provisions for service specified in CCR Ord 24 r 3 (see 6.4) would have to be strictly complied with, so that the proceedings could be brought to the attention of the respondents.

8.18 Application where possession is claimed pursuant to Grounds 1, 3, 4 or 5 of Sched 2 to the Housing Act 1988

Application for accelerated possession following issue of a notice under section 8 of the Housing Act 1988

Claim No.	

In the

County Court

The court office is open from 10am to 4pm Monday to Friday

Telephone

Claimant's full name and address

Name and address for service and payment (if different from above) Ref/Tel no.

Defendant's name (including title, eg Mr, Mrs or Miss) and address

seal

The claimant (your landlord) is claiming possession of

WHAT THIS MEANS

- The court will be deciding whether or not you have to leave, and if you have to leave, when.

You must act immediately - there will not normally be a court hearing.

- **Read this application**, the information leaflet enclosed and the affidavit

- **Get advice** from an advice agency (a list of agencies is attached) or a solicitor

- **Fill in the form of reply** and return it to the court office

Court fee

Solicitor's costs

Total amount

Application issued on

More information about assured tenancies is available in Housing booklet 'Assured and Assured Shorthold Tenancies: A Guide for Tenants'. The booklet is produced by the Department of the Environment. Your local Citizens Advice Bureau will have a copy.

N5A - w3 Application for accelerated possession following issue of a notice under section 8 of the Housing Act 1988 (4.99) *Printed on behalf of The Court Service*

Affidavit to support my application for accelerated possession following issue of a notice under section 8 of the Housing Act 1988 *(The notes in the margin tell you when you have to delete part of the paragraph)*

Paragraph 1
Insert full name, address and occupation of person making this affidavit. Give the address of the property and delete words in brackets to show whether property is a house or part of one

[1]   I,

make this affidavit to support my application for an order for possession of

which is a (dwelling house) (part of a dwelling house).

Paragraph 2
Give the date of the first **written** tenancy agreement. Attach a copy of the agreement to this affidavit. It must contain all the terms of the agreement. Attach also a copy of the latest written agreement

Delete the words in brackets if there was no previous landlord

Delete as appropriate to show whether there is one or more defendant(s). Give date when tenant(s) moved into the property

[2]   On the   day of   [19   ][20   ], I entered into a written tenancy agreement with the defendant(s). A copy of the first agreement, marked 'A', is exhibited (attached) to this affidavit. A copy of the current written agreement, marked 'A1', is also attached.

I confirm that:
* both the tenancy and the agreement were made on or after 15 January 1989.

* I did not let the property mentioned above, or any other property, to the defendant(s) before 15 January 1989, (and neither did any previous landlord).

* the defendant(s) (is) (are) the original tenant(s) to whom the property was let under the assured shorthold tenancy agreement. The tenant(s) first occupied the property on

Paragraph 3
Complete this section only if a new tenancy has been agreed **orally** (not in writing)
Delete the words in brackets if the rent and duration of the tenancy are as set out in the written agreement. If either has changed, delete (i) or (ii) as appropriate

[3]   The current agreement relates to the same, or substantially the same, property. The terms are the same as set out in the agreement at paragraph 2 (except for:

  (i) the amount of rent to be paid. The current rent is

      £   per   ;

  (ii) the duration of the tenancy.)

Paragraph 4
Delete paragraphs (a) or (b) as appropriate to show how the latest tenancy agreement came about

[4]   The tenancy is an assured tenancy.

  (a)   It is subject to the latest written agreement referred to in paragraph 2 above.

  (b)   The latest written agreement referred to in paragraph 2 has expired. There is now a further assured tenancy for an unspecified period. The terms of this tenancy are the same as in the latest written tenancy except as indicated at paragraph 3. Since the latest written agreement, there has not been a tenancy which was agreed orally and which was followed by a statutory periodic tenancy.

Paragraph 5
Delete paragraphs (a)-(c) as appropriate to show the grounds on which you are claiming possession. If paragraph (b) applies, delete the options as applicable to show who bought the property and who intends to live there.

5 The tenancy is an assured tenancy and I am seeking an order for possession on the following grounds:

(a) at some time before the start of the tenancy (I) (a joint landlord) occupied the property as my main home. (The joint landlord's name is   )

(b) I and/or a joint landlord bought the property before the tenancy started and I and/or my spouse, or a joint landlord and/or the joint landlord's spouse, intend(s) to live in it as the main home. (The joint landlord's name is   .)

(c) The tenancy was for a fixed term of eight months or less and, in the twelve months before the tenancy started, the property was let for a holiday.

(d) The tenancy was for a fixed term of twelve months or less and, in the twelve month period before the tenancy started, the property was let to students by a specified educational establishment.

(e) The property is held for use by a minister of religion as a residence from which to carry out (his) (her) duties and is now needed for this purpose.

Paragraph 6
Give the date on which the notice was served. A copy of the notice must be attached to this affidavit

6 A notice was served on the defendant(s) on the   day of   [19   ][20   ] which said I might ask for possession on the ground(s) claimed in paragraph 5. A copy of this notice, marked 'B', is exhibited (attached) to this affidavit.

Paragraph 7
Give details of how the notice (in paragraph 6) was served eg delivered personally, by post, etc. Attach any proof of service eg recorded delivery slip. Mark it 'B1'.

7

Paragraph 8
Give the date on which the notice was served. A copy of the notice must be attached to this affidavit

8 A further notice, under section 8 of the Housing Act 1988, was served on the defendant(s) on the   day of   [19   ][20   ] which said I intended to make an application for possession of the property on the grounds set out in paragraph 5. A copy of this notice, marked 'C', is exhibited (attached) to this affidavit. The notice of   month(s) has expired.

Paragraph 9
Give details of how the notice (in paragraph 8) was served eg delivered personally, by post, etc. Attach any proof of service eg recorded delivery slip. Mark it 'C1'.

9

Paragraph 10
Give details of further evidence (if any) you wish to use to prove your claim for possession under one or more of the grounds set out in paragraph 5. Attach any written document(s) which support that evidence. Mark them 'D1', 'D2' and so on.

10

Paragraph 11
Insert address of property and the time within which you want possession. You must not make any claim for rent arrears

11   I ask the court to grant me an order for possession of

within   days and for payment of my costs of making this application

Sworn at

in the

this   day of   [19   ][20   ]

Before me

Officer of a court appointed
by the Circuit Judge to take affidavits

CERTIFICATE OF SERVICE

I certify that the summons of which this is a true copy was served by me on

by posting it to the Defendant on

at the address stated on the summons

Officer of the Court

I certify that the summons has not been served for the following reasons:

Officer of the Court

8.19 Particulars of claim where possession is claimed pursuant to Ground 13 of Sched 2 to the HA 1988

Particulars of claim

1. The Claimant is the freehold owner of the premises known as and situate at 16 New Road, Gloucester ('the premises').

2. By an oral agreement made on 4 January 1999 the Claimant granted the Defendant a weekly tenancy of the premises at a weekly rent of £60.

3. By reason of the Defendants acts of waste, neglect or default the condition of the premises has deteriorated.

Particulars

(i)   The Defendant has daubed various slogans in paint on the interior walls of the premises;

(ii)   The Defendant has allowed the bath to overflow on numerous occasions, resulting in water seeping through the floorboards and into the underlying plaster damaging the same.

4. By a notice dated 30 April 2000 and served pursuant to s 8 of the Housing Act 1988 the Claimant gave the Defendant notice that proceedings for possession would commence on or after 15 May 1996, and that the Claimant is entitled to possession of the premises by reason of Ground 13 of Schedule 2 to the Housing Act 1988.

5. The Claimant is so entitled to possession of the premises pursuant to the said Ground 13.

6. The Claimant further claims damages for the costs of making good the said acts of waste.

Particulars

(i) Repainting the damaged walls: £100

(ii) Replacing the damaged floorboards: £250

(iii) Replacing the damaged plaster and making good thereafter £300

7. The Claimant claims and is entitled to interest pursuant to s 69 of the County Courts Act 1984.

The Claimant therefore claims:

(i)   possession of the premises;

(ii)   damages;

(iii)   interest pursuant to s 69 of the County Courts Act 1984.

I believe/the Claimant believes the facts stated in these particulars are true.

8.20 Application for accelerated possession where there is an assured shorthold tenancy

Application for accelerated possession following issue of a notice under section 21 of the Housing Act 1988

Claim No.	

In the

County Court

The court office is open from 10am to 4pm Monday to Friday

☎Telephone

Claimant's full name and address

Name and address for service and payment (if different from above) Ref/Tel no.

Defendant's name (including title, eg Mr, Mrs or Miss) and address

seal

The claimant (your landlord) is claiming possession of

WHAT THIS MEANS

- The court will be deciding whether or not you have to leave, and if you have to leave, when.

You must act immediately - there will not normally be a court hearing.

- **Read this application**, the information leaflet enclosed and the affidavit

- **Get advice** from an advice agency (a list of agencies is attached) or a solicitor

- **Fill in the form of reply** and return it to the court office

Court fee	
Solicitor's costs	
Total amount	
Application issued on	

More information about assured tenancies is available in Housing booklet 'Assured and Assured Shorthold Tenancies: A Guide for Tenants'. The booklet is produced by the Department of the Environment. Your local Citizens Advice Bureau will have a copy.

N5B Application for accelerated possession following issue of a notice under section 21 of the Housing Act 1988 (10.00)   *Printed on behalf of The Court Service*

Affidavit to support my application for accelerated possession following issue of a notice under section 21 of the Housing Act 1988 *(The notes in the margin tell you when you have to delete part of the paragraph)*

Paragraph 1
Insert full name, address and occupation of person making this affidavit. Give the address of the property and delete words in brackets to show whether property is a house or part of one

1 I,

make this affidavit to support my application for an order for possession

of

which is a (dwelling house) (part of a dwelling house).

Paragraph 2
Give the date of the first **written** tenancy agreement. Attach a copy of the agreement to this affidavit. It must contain all the terms of the agreement. Attach also a copy of the latest written agreement

Delete the words in brackets if there was no previous landlord

Delete as appropriate, to show whether there is one or more defendants. Give date when tenant(s) moved into the property

2 On the   day of   [19   ][20   ], I entered into a written tenancy agreement with the defendant(s). A copy of the first agreement, marked 'A', is exhibited (attached) to this affidavit. A copy of the current written agreement, marked 'A1', is also attached.

I confirm that:
- both the tenancy and the agreement were made on or after 15 January 1989.

- I did not let the property mentioned above, or any other property, to the defendant(s) before 15 January 1989, (and neither did any previous landlord).

- the defendant(s) (is) (are) the original tenant(s) to whom the property was let under the assured shorthold tenancy agreement. The tenant(s) first occupied the property on

Paragraph 3
Complete this section only if a new tenancy has been agreed **orally** (not in writing)
Delete the words in brackets if the rent and duration of the tenancy are as set out in the written agreement. If either has changed, delete (i) or (ii) as appropriate

3 The current agreement relates to the same, or substantially the same, property. The terms are the same as set out in the agreement at paragraph 2 (except for:

(i) the amount of rent to be paid. The current rent is

£   per   ;

(ii) the duration of the tenancy.)

Paragraph 4
Delete paragraphs (a) or (b) as appropriate to show how the latest tenancy agreement came about
If the tenancy is different from either of these two categories, you cannot use the Accelerated Possession Procedure

4 The tenancy is an assured shorthold tenancy.

(a)   The latest written agreement referred to in paragraph 2 has expired. There is now a further assured shorthold tenancy for an unspecified period. The terms of this tenancy are the same as in the latest written tenancy except as indicated at paragraph 3. Since the latest written agreement, there has not been a tenancy which was agreed orally and which was followed by a statutory periodic tenancy.

(b)   It is subject to the latest written agreement referred to in paragraph 2 above, and it is not for a fixed term.

Paragraph 5

5 The assured shorthold tenancy did not follow an assured non-shorthold tenancy.

Paragraph 6

6 I did not serve a notice on the defendant(s) before the previous assured shorthold tenancy expired, saying that any new tenancy would not be an assured shorthold tenancy, nor did the tenancy agreement contain a provision saying it was not an assured shorthold tenancy, nor is the tenancy an assured non-shorthold tenancy under any other provision of Schedule 2A to the Housing Act 1988.

Paragraph 7
Delete this paragraph if the tenancy and/or any agreement for it was entered into on or after 28 February 1997

7 A notice, under section 20 of the Housing Act 1988, was served on the defendant(s) on the   day of   [19   ][20   ] which said that the tenancy was to be an assured shorthold tenancy. A copy of this notice, marked 'B', is exhibited (attached) to this affidavit.

Paragraph 8
Give details of how the notice (in paragraph 7) was served eg delivered personally, by post, etc. Attach any proof of service eg recorded delivery slip. Mark it 'B1'.

8

Paragraph 9
Give the date on which the notice was served and the length of notice given. A copy of the notice must be attached to this affidavit

9 A notice, under section 21 of the Housing Act 1988, was served on the defendant(s) on the   day of   [19   ][20   ] which said possession of the property was required. A copy of that notice, marked 'C', is exhibited (attached) to this affidavit. The notice of   month(s) has expired.

Paragraph 10
Give details of how the notice (in paragraph 9) was served eg delivered personally, by post, etc. Attach any proof of service eg recorded delivery slip. Mark it 'C1'.

10

Paragraph 11
Give details of further
evidence (if any) you wish
to use to prove your claim
for possession. Attach any
written document(s) which
support that evidence.
Mark them 'D1', 'D2' and
so on

[11]

Paragraph 12
Insert address of property
and the time within which
you want possession. You
must not make any claim for
rent arrears

[12] I ask the court to grant me an order for possession of

within   days and for payment of my costs of making this application

Paragraph 13
If the court is satisfied
that the defendant would
suffer exceptional
hardship the period can be
extended for up to 6
weeks, but no longer. The
court may make this
decision without a hearing.

[13] If the defendant seeks a postponement of possession on the grounds of exceptional hardship,
do you wish to attend any hearing the judge may hold to consider the request?

☐ Yes   ☐ No

Sworn at

in the

this   day of   [19   ][20   ]

Before me

*Officer of a court appointed
by the Circuit Judge to take affidavits*

CERTIFICATE OF SERVICE

I certify that the summons of which this is a true copy was served by me on

by posting it to the Defendant on

at the address stated on the summons

Officer of the Court

I certify that the summons has not been served for the following reasons:

Officer of the Court

9 Related Areas

Like most areas of law residential tenancies overlap with several other areas. The client seeking advice on a problem which has led to recourse to this book may also need to be advised on a number of other matters. Those which are most likely to be useful are discussed in the briefest outline below.

9.1 Public sector housing

Tenancies granted by local authorities, housing associations and other public or charitable bodies are generally outside the scope of the Rent Act 1977 and the parts of the Housing Act 1988 which have been discussed in this book. They are referred to as secure tenancies and are regulated by the Housing Act 1985. On terminating such a tenancy, the landlord must give to the tenant a notice of termination stating the grounds on which the court will be asked to make a possession order. There is a degree of overlap between the grounds on which a court can make an order for possession in respect of a secure tenancy and the grounds on which it can do so in respect of a protected or statutory tenancy. A full explanation of the procedure for obtaining possession and the appropriate grounds will be found in, for instance, Webber and Davidson or Arden and Partington (see below, 11.2).

Sometimes, a tenant against whom a possession order is sought is willing to have such an order made against him as he believes that he will then be entitled to council housing, the local authority being unable to treat him as voluntarily homeless, as it could do if he left without a court order. Such assumptions are not always correct. Before advising a client in those circumstances, a check should be made with the relevant local authority about their policy.

9.2   Housing benefit

Many tenants are entitled to receive housing benefit from their local authority in respect of all or part of their rent. The exact entitlement is calculated with regard to the amount of rent the tenant has to pay, the number of dependants he has and his earnings. Where the tenant is in receipt of supplementary benefit, the full amount of his rent should be paid through the DSS. With the agreement of the tenant, this benefit may be payable directly to the landlord. Amongst tenants who are on relatively low incomes and who would be entitled to housing benefit, there is a surprisingly high degree of ignorance about this benefit. Generally, it may help a tenant seeking advice on landlord and tenant matters to have the existence of housing benefit pointed out to him. More information can be found in the Child Poverty Action Group's guide (see 11.2).

9.3   Tenancies of business premises

These tenancies qualify for a different form of protection which is given by Part II of the Landlord and Tenant Act 1954. Where premises are let for both residential and business purposes, the provisions of the 1954 Act will apply rather than the Rent Acts and Housing Act unless the business use is ancillary to the residential use, for example, *Wright v Mortimer* [1996] EGCS 51, CA. There is no control of the rent payable on the original granting of a business tenancy, although the court may determine the rate for subsequent tenancies. The landlord must renew the tenancy at the end of its term unless certain circumstances apply. If the tenancy is not renewed through no fault of the tenant, he will be entitled to compensation.

9.4   Agricultural tenancies

The law relating to tenancies let along with agricultural land or to agricultural employees is exceptionally complex. Some, but not all of these tenancies are capable of being protected or assured tenancies (see 2.3.7). Even if they are protected tenancies, there are circumstances unique to such tenancies where the landlord may be able to recover possession against the tenant. A full discussion of agricultural tenancies can be found in Webber and Davidson (see 11.2).

9.5   Long leases

A long tenancy is one originally granted for a term of 21 years or more, at a rent not less than two-thirds of the rateable value. Such a tenancy will not be a protected tenancy. There is no prohibition on charging a premium on the assignment of such a tenancy. Indeed, the vast majority of flats which are 'owner occupied' are let on such leases. In some circumstances, the tenant on the expiry of such a lease will be able to extend the lease or acquire the freehold pursuant to the Leasehold Reform Act 1967. These provisions have been supplemented by the Leasehold Reform, Housing and Urban Development Act 1993 which gave further rights of lease renewal for tenants of flats. Even if those provisions and 'leasehold enfranchisement', which is also provided for in both Acts, do not apply, the landlord's right to possession at the expiry of the lease is restricted by Pt I of the Landlord and Tenant Act 1954.

10 Common Practical Problems

10.1

My client is going to work abroad for two years. He wants to let out his home whilst he is away, but wants to be able to recover possession when he returns home without any difficulties. What is the best way to be sure he will be able to accomplish this?

Advice:

He would probably do best to grant a tenancy of the property which is subject to Case 1 of Sched 2 to the Housing Act 1988, on the basis of his previous residence there. Before granting the tenancy, he must serve the tenant with a notice telling him that the tenancy is to be subject to this Ground and should get the tenant to sign a receipt for that notice (see 2.9.1 and 6.5.1). He will then be able to recover possession whenever he wants, subject only to giving two months' notice pursuant to s 8. It will not be necessary for him to show any reason for requiring possession before exercising this right. Although he could achieve the same ability to recover the property by granting an assured shorthold tenancy without serving the Ground 1 notice, using the notice gives him the advantage of being able to use summary procedure (see 6.8).

10.2

I have been consulted by a tenant who wants to know if his landlord is entitled to raise the rent on his flat. Is the landlord entitled to do this?

Advice:

First establish whether the tenancy was granted before the commencement date of the Housing Act 1988 (15 January 1989). If it was granted before that date, next establish whether there is a fair rent registered in respect of the flat. The tenant may know the answer himself. If he doesn't know, the local rent officer (generally listed in telephone directories under 'Rent Officer') will tell you. If there is a registered rent, the landlord can only raise the rent to that which has been registered. If two years have passed since the last registration, he is entitled to apply for it to be reassessed (see 4.2.5). If there is no registered rent and the tenancy has always been a periodic one, the landlord can charge what he likes, subject to any contractual restraint. If the tenancy has become a statutory one, the landlord must first serve a notice of increase as prescribed in s 45 of the Rent Act 1977 (see 4.2.5). In any case, if the tenant feels that he is being overcharged, he should make an application for a fair rent to be assessed.

If the tenancy was granted on or after 15 January 1989, the landlord must first serve a notice that he intends increasing the rent pursuant to s 13 of the Housing Act 1988. The tenant is then entitled to refer the notice to a rent assessment committee who can decide by how much, if anything, the rent should be increased. The rent assessed by this committee is, however, likely to be higher than the rent a rent officer would register as a 'fair rent'.

10.3

My client has recently inherited a house that is the subject of a long standing Rent Act tenancy. Although he believes the present tenants are satisfactory, he would like to be able to obtain possession, as he wishes to live there himself. Can he do this?

Advice:

The court can make a possession order under Case 9 of Sched 15 to the Rent Act 1977 on the grounds that the landlord wishes to live there himself unless the landlord acquired his interest by purchase, which someone who inherits a property, of course, does not do. The court will, however, order possession only if it considers it reasonable to do so (see 6.2). Where there are long standing tenants, and the landlord has his own accommodation, it is unlikely that the court would make such an order. The court might be more inclined to do so if the landlord were in a position to offer the tenants suitable alternative accommodation, in which case s 98(1)(a) of the 1977 Act might apply (see 6.2.14).

10.4

I was consulted yesterday by a landlord who is anxious to regain possession of premises recently let to a tenant who persistently holds noisy parties. He wrote a letter to the tenant a month ago telling him he must leave. Can he start proceedings yet?

Advice:

Normally a court will only order possession if a valid notice pursuant to s 8 of the Housing Act 1988 has been served (see 6.7). It does not sound as if this letter constituted a proper notice. Such a notice must contain prescribed information. Once the notice has been served, as the possession claim will be based on Ground 14 proceedings can be served immediately. If proceedings had been commenced without the service of a notice, the court would have had a discretion to start proceedings. If the tenancy had been granted before 15 January 1989 and had continued as a periodic tenancy since then, the landlord would have to serve a notice to quit in the prescribed form before commencing proceedings and there would be no power to dispense with that notice.

10.5

I have been consulted by some students from the local university. Three months ago they were granted what their landlord described as a 'student tenancy'. The landlord has now decided that he wants to evict them. He has not given any reason for this. He has told them that as they are students, they do not have any rights as tenants. Is this correct?

Advice:

It seems likely that your clients are in fact assured shorthold tenants. Students are, of course, entitled to the same rights as anyone else. The only exception is where the tenancy has been granted by a specified educational institution or body of persons (Sched 1, para 8 of the HA 1988) (see 6.5.3). This provision applies only if the tenants are students, but regardless of whether they are studying at the institution which granted the tenancy. If para 8 does apply, then the landlord will be entitled to possession once the contractual term of the tenancy has expired, though will still have to obtain a court order.

10.6

I have a client who is a shopkeeper and who owns the flat above his shop. He would like to let the flat out, but wants to be sure of being able to recover possession of it as he expects to sell the shop and flat in a couple of years. What is the best thing for him to do?

Advice:

If he grants an assured shorthold tenancy of the property, he will have an indisputable right to possession (see 2.6). This must be for at least six months. There is no longer any requirement for the landlord to provide any notice saying it is to be an assured shorthold. At the expiry of the term, the landlord will be able to recover possession relatively simply and cheaply (see 6.8 for the procedure). The fact that the landlord owns the premises below the flat will not affect the position, as they are not his residence.

10.7

My clients have been given a notice to quit by their landlord. He has told them that they are not tenants and only have a 'licence'. The reason he gives for this is that he lives in the top floor flat of the same house, which has four storeys. My clients live in the self-contained basement flat. Is what the landlord says correct, and if it is, do my clients have any protection from being evicted?

Advice:

Assuming the agreement was entered into after 15 January 1989, the 'tenants' will have virtually no rights in this situation. The question of whether they are tenants or licensees is fairly academic. If there is a tenancy, it will not be given any statutory protection by reason of para 10 of Sched 1 to the Housing Act 1988. This provides that where landlord and tenant live in the same building, even in different self-contained flats (unless it is a purpose built block), the landlord will be able to obtain possession so long as the contractual term and/or a valid notice to quit have expired.

In the rare case of such an occupancy having commenced before the commencement of the Housing Act 1988, the court has a discretion to postpone the coming into force of any notice to quit by up to three months.

10.8

In 1988, my client granted a 'Case 11' tenancy of premises he had previously resided at four years previously. He now wishes to repossess those premises so that he can live there. The tenant claims he was served with the Case 11 notice only after the tenancy commenced and that therefore, there is no right to possession. The tenant has accepted in an open letter written to us that the effect of a Case 11 notice was explained to him orally before the tenancy commenced. In any event, our file indicates that the tenant did receive the notice before the commencement of the tenancy. Is our client likely to be able to recover possession, and how should we proceed?

Advice:

If the court finds that the notice was not served, then it still has a discretion to order possession. With events so long ago, what is recorded on a solicitor's file may carry more weight than the tenant's recollection. The circumstances you have indicated would probably lead the court to exercise its discretion in favour of the landlord, regardless of whether it found as a fact that the notice had been served.

11 Further Reading

11.1 Major works

There are two major looseleaf works on the entire field of landlord and tenant law, which together with *Megarry*, the one – bound – major work on residential tenancies, are regarded by most practitioners in the area as being the primary sources.

Hill and Redman, *Landlord and Tenant,* London: Butterworths. A four volume work with a separate index, covering all aspects of landlord and tenant law. Usually updated three times a year.

Megarry, The Rent Acts Assured Tenancies, 11th edn, 1987, with 1993 supplement. Now brought up to date by a useful, though grossly overpriced, second edition of the third volume by Timothy Fancourt, known as *Megarry's Assured Tenancies.*

Woodfall's Law of Landlord and Tenant, 28th edn, London: Sweet & Maxwell. A four volume work with a separate index, covering all aspects of landlord and tenant law. Two or three updates a year.

11.2 Books

Other books on the areas covered by this book and related areas that may be of assistance:

Aldridge's Residential Lettings, 11th edn, 1998, London: Sweet & Maxwell. A reasonably full guide to this area of the law.

Arden and Partington, *Housing Law*, 2nd edn, 1994, London: Sweet & Maxwell. This regularly updated, looseleaf work brings together the mass of law – public and private – relating to the regulation of housing.

Bean, D, *Injunctions*, 8th edn, 2000, London: Sweet & Maxwell. Concise, but still regarded by many practitioners as the most helpful book on the subject.

Bridge, S, *Assured Tenancies*, 1999, London: Blackstone. A thoroughly competent account of the relevant law.

Bridge, S, *Statutes on Landlord and Tenant*, 3rd edn, 1999, London: Blackstone. Far better value than Butterworths' *Handbook*.

Butterworths Residential Landlord and Tenant Handbook, 2nd edn, 1998. Contains all the legislation, primary and secondary, governing this area.

Child Poverty Action Group, *Housing Benefit and Council Tax Legislation*. Published annually. The most usable guide to these benefits.

Colbey, R, *Resident Landlords and Owner-Occupiers: Law and Practice*, 1987, Longman/FT Law & Tax. Deals with tenancies where granted by resident landlords and the Rent Act 1977.

Harpum, C, *Megarry and Wade's Law of Real Property*, 6th edn, 2000, London: Sweet & Maxwell. A standard work which deals with many areas that are of practical importance in the landlord and tenant field.

Matthews, A, *The Landlords' and Tenants' Handbook*, 1995, Fitzwarren. A simple guide to residential tenancies, bridging the gap between legal textbooks and laymen's guides.

McGregor, H, *Damages*, 16th edn, 1997, London: Sweet & Maxwell. The leading textbook on damages.

O'Hare and Hill, *Civil Litigation*, 9th edn, 2000. A comprehensive, yet simple and reasonably priced guide to most forms of civil proceedings; of great assistance to the practitioner in many areas, of which landlord and tenant is just one.

Webber and Davidson, *Residential Possession Proceedings*, 5th edn, 1997, London: Sweet & Maxwell. A comprehensive guide to all forms of residential possession proceedings including areas outside the scope of this book, such as agricultural tenancies, public sector tenancies and mortgages.

11.3 Other sources of information

The Civil Court Practice, which has effectively replaced the County Court Practice and remains known as the 'Green Book', contains sections on residential tenancies, somewhat reduced from the form they took in the old work. The indexation and layout improved a little for the 2000 edition after the disastrous production in 1999, but still leave a lot to be desired. It is still of considerable help to the practitioner, particularly on the procedural aspects of bringing a possession claim. *Blackstone's Civil Practice* is becoming a serious rival to the Green Book and has an equally useful section on landlord and tenant.

The major law reports (The Law Reports, Weekly Law Reports and All England Law Reports) should carry the most important landlord and tenant cases. The Estates Gazette, the Property and Compensation Reports and the Housing Law Reports are all of particular value in this area.

Rent officers and leasehold valuation tribunals should be able to provide helpful pamphlets on many aspects of landlord and tenant law.